D1084548

Jane Austen

Her Homes
& Her Friends

Jane Austen

Jane Austen

Her Homes & Her Friends

Constance Hill

Illustrated by
Ellen G. Hill

Dover Publications, Inc.
Mineola, New York

Bibliographical Note

This Dover edition, first published in 2018, is an unabridged republication of the edition first published by John Lane, The Bodley Head Limited, London, in 1923.

Library of Congress Cataloging-in-Publication Data

Names: Hill, Constance, 1844?–1929, author. | Hill, Ellen G., illustrator.
Title: Jane Austen : her homes and her friends / Constance Hill ; illustrated by Ellen G. Hill.
Description: Mineola, New York : Dover Publications, Inc., 2018.
Identifiers: LCCN 2018021342| ISBN 9780486826769 | ISBN 0486826767
Subjects: LCSH: Austen, Jane, 1775—1817—Homes and haunts. | Austen, Jane, 1775—1817—Friends and associates. | Novelists, English—Homes and haunts—England. | Novelists, English—19th century—Biography. | England—Intellectual life—19th century. | Literary landmark—England.
Classification: LCC PR4036 .H5 2018 | DDC 823/.7 [BJ—dc23
LC record available at https://lccn.loc.gov/2018021342

Manufactured in the United States by LSC Communications
82676701   2018
www.doverpublications.com

PREFACE TO THIRD EDITION

In introducing a third edition of this work to the public, it is a satisfaction to reflect that since its first appearance, followed by other works by other authors on the same subject, the love and appreciation of Jane Austen's writings have spread wider and wider throughout the English-speaking world.

On the centenary of Miss Austen's death, which occurred on July 18th, 1917, an interesting little ceremony took place at Chawton, Hants, where a Tablet had been placed on the walls of Chawton Cottage, her last home, and whence all her works were sent into the world.

The Tablet of solid oak, designed by my sister, Miss E. G. Hill, suggests by its ornamentation subjects connected with the life of the authoress. Thus its framework represents that of a window in 4 Sydney Place, Bath, where the Austen family lived from 1801 till 1804, and the delicate, raised pattern that encircles the bronze plate bearing the inscription is copied from embroidery on a muslin scarf worked by Jane herself.

Preface to Third Edition

The inscription runs as follows :—

JANE AUSTEN

lived here from 1809 to 1817
and hence all her works
were sent into the world.
Her admirers in this country
and in America have united
to erect this Tablet.

. . .

"Such art as hers can never grow old."

Happy were those of us who were able to be present at the unveiling of the Tablet! Several members of the Austen family were there, including the present owner of Chawton House, a descendant of Jane's brother Edward, who took the name of Knight.

We found the little parlour on the right-hand side of the entrance door gay with country flowers in honour of the day. There in that room were written " Mansfield Park," " Emma," and " Persuasion," so that we, her grateful readers from far and near, were standing on the very spot where Jane sat at her little mahogany desk and brought into being the gentle Fanny Price, the spirited Emma, and the sweet Anne Elliot. The speeches were from the heart, and warm in

Preface to Third Edition

appreciation of one who had bestowed upon us a "perennial joy."

The subscriptions for the Memorial were so numerous and generous that after the expenses of the Tablet were defrayed there remained a goodly sum in our hands with which to benefit the village of Steventon, Miss Austen's birthplace. Accordingly an excellent "Young People's Library," bearing her name, was presented to that place, to which several publishers kindly contributed books.

I should like to close this short Preface with some words of Dr. Johnson's, peculiarly applicable to Jane Austen:

"To be able to furnish pleasure that is harmless pleasure, pure and unalloyed, is as great a power as man can possess."

CONSTANCE HILL.

GROVE COTTAGE, FROGNAL, HAMPSTEAD.
March 1923.

PREFACE TO FIRST EDITION

It has been remarked that " in works of genius there is always something intangible—something that can be *felt* but that cannot be clearly defined —something that eludes us when we attempt to put it into words." This "intangible something" —this undefinable charm—is felt by all Jane Austen's admirers. It has exercised a sway of ever-increasing power over the writer and illustrator of these pages ; constraining them to follow the author to all the places where she dwelt and inspiring them with a determination to find out all that could be known of her life and its surroundings.

Such a pilgrimage in the footprints of a favourite writer would, alas ! in many cases lead to a sad disenchantment, but no such pain awaits those who follow Miss Austen's gentle steps. The more intimate their knowledge of her character becomes the more must they admire and love her rare spirit and the more thorough must be their enjoyment in her racy humour—a humour which makes everything she touches delightful, but which never degenerates into caricature nor into "jestings which are not convenient." Elizabeth Bennet is speaking in the author's own person when she says to Darcy: "I hope I never ridicule what is wise or good. Follies and nonsense, whims and inconsistencies *do* divert me, I own, and I laugh at them whenever I can." We read in a short memoir of Miss Austen written by her brother Henry, "Though the frailties, foibles and follies of others could not escape her immediate detection, yet even on their vices did she never trust herself to comment with unkindness. . . . She always sought in the faults of others something to excuse, to forgive or forget."

"Her own family were so much and the rest of the world so little to Jane Austen" that it is in the centre of that family that we can best study her character and learn to recognise the influences which affected her as a writer. For she was not amongst those authors who have unveiled in their letters their innermost thoughts and feelings. "With all the playful frankness of her manner," writes a niece, "her sweet sunny temper and enthusiastic nature, Jane Austen was a woman most reticent as to her own deepest and holiest feelings." And it is, therefore, by seeing her

Preface to First Edition

nature reflected, as it were, in those around her, and by finding out gradually the place she held in their midst, that we learn to know her better. We are thus enabled, too, to trace the connection between the author's individual experience and that of the personages in her novels—personages who are so real to her readers that their characters and actions are debated by admirers and non-admirers alike as those of beings who have actually walked this earth. " Is there any other writer," asks a critic, " in whom men and women can take an equal interest and discuss on equal terms?" But her charm, as we have said, is too impalpable to be argued about and so, as another critic remarks, "the only homage her vassals can pay her in the face of the enemy is to lose their tempers."

Through the kindness of members of various branches of the Austen family we have had access to interesting manuscripts recording the home life at Steventon, at Chawton and elsewhere, and giving a picture also of the happy intercourse between "Aunt Jane" and the many young nephews and nieces with whom she was always "the centre of attraction." In addition to this we have had the loan of family portraits and pictures, as well as of contemporary sketches representing places associated with her which either no longer exist or are greatly altered. With this help it has been

Preface to First Edition

possible to reconstruct much which at first sight seemed to be irrecoverably lost.

We would now request our readers, in imagination, to put back the finger of Time for more than a hundred years and to step with us into Miss Austen's presence. "No one," writes her brother, "could be often in her company without feeling a strong desire of obtaining her friendship, and cherishing a hope of having obtained it." That friendship seems to be extended to all who, whether through her works, her biographies or her letters, can "hold communion sweet" with the mind and with the heart of Jane Austen.

CONSTANCE HILL.

GROVE COTTAGE, FROGNAL, HAMPSTEAD.
September 1901.

CONTENTS

xiii

Contents

LIST OF ILLUSTRATIONS

List of Illustrations

List of Illustrations

List of Illustrations

Jane Austen

Her Homes
& Her Friends

CHAPTER I

AN ARRIVAL IN AUSTEN-LAND

On a fine morning, in the middle of September, a country chaise was threading its way through Hampshire lanes. In it were seated two ardent admirers of Jane Austen, armed with pen and pencil who were eager to see the places where she dwelt, to look upon the scenes that she had looked upon, and to learn all that could be learnt of her surroundings.

The chaise in question had been hired in a country village from a blacksmith, and was driven by the blacksmith's wife. The good woman knew little more than we (the travellers) did of the cross-country journey of twenty-two miles that lay before us. Still, there would be finger-posts to direct us and, no doubt, wayfarers to be questioned ; and in the meantime our sturdy pony trotted so briskly along that he seemed ready to accomplish a yet longer journey.

We had studied the map and fancied that by various short cuts we could accomplish the drive before nightfall. But alas for short cuts! We were puzzled at the very first choice of byways! There was nothing for it but to inquire at a group of roadside cottages. So one of us walked up a garden glowing with late summer flowers and tapped at the entrance-door. No answer came from within, so we tried another—flanked with laden apple-trees—and another and another, with no better success. Then it occurred to us that the inhabitants must be all away hop-gathering. We had, indeed, left the villagers hard at work at our starting-point, where the parson's young daughter had joined one of the groups and was busy helping some old women to fill their sacks.

How beautiful were those narrow lanes through which we passed, with their hedgerows of arching trees and their steep banks adorned with yellow bracken and the long sprays of blackberry-bushes covered with ripening fruit! The immediate goal of this journey was none other than Steventon— the birthplace of Jane Austen ; but Steventon, it seemed, was a village where no lodging was to be had, and we had been advised to halt at Clarken Green, a hamlet within a few miles of Steventon, where we might sleep at a small country tavern. For Clarken Green, therefore, we were bound.

Once we asked our way of a field labourer we chanced to meet, but found that he was unaware

An Arrival in Austen-land

of the very existence of Clarken Green. At last, having arrived at something of a village, a good-natured innkeeper standing in the midst of his pigeons and poultry, entered into our difficulties ; told us that we had come far out of our way and advised our making for the Basingstoke road. This, with the aid of his directions, we succeeded in doing, and towards evening found ourselves entering the old town of Basingstoke. After a short halt we again resumed our journey, and finally, as darkness was closing in, we drew up triumphantly at the solitary inn of Clarken Green.

But our triumph was of short duration. Within doors all was confusion—rooms dismantled, packing-cases choking up the entries, and furniture piled up against the walls. The innkeeper and his family, we found, were on the eve of a departure. It was impossible, he said, to receive us, but he offered us the use of a chaise and a fresh horse to take us on to Deane—a place a few miles farther west—where he thought it possible we might find shelter in a small inn. The name struck our ears, for Deane has its associations with the Austen family. There Jane's father and mother spent the first seven years of their married life. By all means let us go to Deane ! So bidding farewell to our charioteer, the blacksmith's wife, as she led her sturdy pony into the stable, we drove off cheerily along the darkening roads. Before long a light appeared between the trees, and in a few minutes we were stopping in front of a low, rambling, whitewashed building—the small wayside inn of Deane Gate.

Our troubles were now over, and much we enjoyed our cosy supper, which we ate in a tiny parlour of spotless cleanliness. A chat with our landlady gave us the welcome intelligence that we were within two miles of Steventon. Our small tavern and Gatehouse (as it was formerly) stood, she said, where the lane for Steventon joins the main road to the west. This, no doubt, would give it importance for the Austens and their country neighbours ; and we recalled the words of Jane in one of her letters, when speaking of a drive from Basingstoke to Steventon she says: " We left Warren at Dean Gate on our way home." So we fell asleep that night with the happy consciousness that we were really in Austen-land.

CHAPTER II

STEVENTON

" By hedge-row elms on hillocks green."

THE sun shone brightly on our first morning in Austen-land, and showed us that we were in a peaceful country of green pastures and low wooded hills. My companion was soon seated by the roadside making a sketch of the inn, whilst I took a hurried peep at the small village of Deane and at Deane Manor House, a fine seventeenth-century building, whose grounds adjoin the churchyard. But we shall return to Deane later on, and must now hasten to Steventon. The chaise that brought us from Clarken Green last evening is waiting to take us there.

As we drive along Deane Lane we think of the family party which made that same journey a hundred and thirty years ago. When Mr. and Mrs. George Austen quitted Deane in 1771, to make their home at Steventon, Deane Lane "was a mere cart track, so cut up by deep

ruts as to be impassable for a light carriage.
Mrs. Austen, who was not then in strong health,

THE DEANE GATE

performed the short journey on a feather bed,
placed upon some soft articles of furniture in the
waggon which held their household goods." *

* " Memoir of Jane Austen." by J. E. Austen-Leigh.

Steventon

We seem to see the quaint caravan moving in front of us, as we follow the same track and look, as the Austens did, upon the green slopes of Ashe Park on either side of the lane.

Leaving the park, the road turns abruptly to the right, and we find ourselves entering the sunny village of Steventon, which lies in a gentle hollow. We alight from our chaise and walk between the gardens of pretty cottages that border the road. These cottages, it seems, form the village, and passing them we proceed along Steventon Lane. A knoll, on the left, is surmounted by the new rectory, and on the right, green fields and woods cover a hillside, on the top of which, we are told, we shall find the church. Presently we reach a meadow at the foot of the hill and notice that the ground slopes up to a grassy terrace. This is the place! We cannot mistake it. This is the site of the old parsonage-house where Jane Austen was born! For her nephew tells us that "along the upper or southern side of the garden ran a terrace of the finest turf." There is the very terrace described! We know that the house stood between it and the lane, but what is the exact site? Can no one tell us? May there not be some person yet living who remembers the parsonage pulled down in 1826?

Inspired by this idea, we hurry back to the cottages and speculate upon each open door as to what might be gained from its dark interior. At last we see an old man leaning on his garden-gate.

" Can you tell us," we anxiously inquire, " where the old parsonage stood in which the Austen family lived long ago ? "

" Ay, that I can," he exclaims : "maybe you've seen the field at the corner where the church lane cooms out o' Steventon Lane ? Well, if you saw that, did you notice a pump in the middle o' the field ? "

" Yes, yes ! "

" Well, that pump stood i' the washhouse at the back o' the parsonage. There's a well under the pump. The Austens got their water from that well. I was a little 'un when the old house was pulled down, but I well recollect seeing all the bricks and rubbish lyin' about on the ground."

" The house faced the road, did it not ? " we ask.

" Yes ; and the gates o' the drive were at the corner o' the field, between the church lane and Steventon Lane. I remember when you could make out the line o' the drive quite well, 'cause the grass grew poor and thin where the gravel had been."

Presently we learn that our informant's grand-father, whose name was Littlewart, was coachman to Mr. James Austen, Jane's eldest brother.

Steventon

"I used to hear a deal about the Austens when I was a lad," continued our friend, "from my

THE SITE OF THE OLD PARSONAGE, STEVENTON

mother, for she was a god-daughter o' Miss Jane's. People tell me now that Miss Jane wrote some fine stories, and I've just seen her name in a newspaper. I'll go and fetch the paper for you to see." And the old man hurries into his cottage.

Whilst he is away I refer to a volume of Jane Austen's Letters which I carry under my arm, to see if, by chance, the name of Littlewart occurs in any of them. Yes! here it is in one dated November 1798. Jane is writing from Steventon to a sister-in-law, and after telling her that " their family affairs are somewhat deranged" owing to illness among the servants, she goes on to say: " You and Edward will be amused, I think, when you know that Nanny Littlewart dresses my hair." It was evidently this Nanny Littlewart's daughter that was godchild to Jane Austen. So we have been actually talking to the son of her god-daughter!

After showing proper appreciation of the newspaper paragraph, we return to the meadow where the parsonage stood. My companion sits down on a bank to sketch the terrace and the pump, for the pump, barely noticed before, has become interesting now as the only visible relic of the Austens' home. Meanwhile I wander over the field endeavouring to

> " Summon from the shadowy past
> The forms that once have been."

I can now picture to myself the exact spot

where the parsonage stood, and can fancy the
carriage drive approaching it "between turf and
trees" from the gates at the corner of the two
lanes. I can even fancy the house itself, being
familiar with two old pencil views of it taken by
members of the Austen family. These show that
the front had a latticed porch, and that the back

STEVENTON PARSONAGE (FRONT VIEW)

had two projecting wings and looked on to the
garden which sloped up to the terrace "walk."
In both sketches fine trees are introduced, and as
I saunter about I notice some great flat stumps of
elm-trees in the grass. The sight of these brings
to mind a letter of Jane's, written in November
1800, in which she says: "We have had a dread-
ful storm of wind in the fore part of this day,
which has done a great deal of mischief among
our trees. I was sitting alone in the dining-room

when an odd kind of crash startled me; in a moment afterwards it was repeated. I then went to the window, which I reached just in time to see the last of our two highly-valued elms descend into the Sweep!!!! The other, which had fallen, I suppose, in the first crash, and which was the nearest to the pond, taking a more easterly direction, sank among our screen of chestnuts and firs, knocking down one spruce fir, beating off the head of another, and stripping the two corner chestnuts of several branches in its fall. This is not all. One large elm, out of the two on the left-hand side as you enter what I call the elm walk, was likewise blown down; the maple bearing the weathercock was broke in two, and what I regret more than all the rest is, that all the three elms which grew in Hall's meadow, and gave such ornament to it, are gone; two were blown down, and the other so much injured that it cannot stand. I am happy to add," she continues, "that no greater evil than the loss of trees has been the consequence of the storm in this place, or in our immediate neighbourhood. We grieve therefore in some comfort." *

The "elm walk" alluded to, which is sometimes called the "wood walk" in the "Letters," extended from the terrace westward and led to a rustic shrubbery. The shrubbery has disappeared,

* "Memoir," by J. E. Austen-Leigh.

but there are groups of trees on the slope of the

ENTRANCE TO STEVENTON CHURCH

terrace that may have shaded the " walk." One group is especially beautiful. It consists of tall sycamores with their pale grey stems and dark

Jane Austen

green foliage, among which an old thorn has entwined its branches. We read in one of the "Letters" from Steventon : "The bank along the elm walk is sloped down for the reception of thorns and lilacs."

Perhaps these features of her home may have been in the author's mind when she described "Cleveland" in "Sense and Sensibility." "It had no park, but the pleasure grounds were tolerably extensive. . . . It had its open shrubbery and closer wood walk. . . . The house itself was under the guardianship of the fir, the mountain ash, and the acacia."

The ground between the house and the terrace "was occupied by one of those old-fashioned gardens in which vegetables and flowers are combined, flanked and protected on the east by one of the thatched mud walls common in that country, and overshadowed by fine elms."* I look on the sloping grass "where once *this* garden smiled," and fancy I see fruit-trees and flowers and that I even catch a glimpse of two girlish forms moving among them—those of Jane Austen and her sister Cassandra ; that only sister so dear to the heart of Jane, of whom she spoke, "even in the maturity of her powers, as of one wiser and better than herself."

We are told that a path called the "Church

* "Memoir," by J. E. Austen-Leigh.

14

THE SQUIRE'S PEW

walk" started from the eastern end of the terrace
and ascended the steep hill behind the parsonage
to the church. It ran between "hedgerows under
whose shelter the earliest primroses, anemones,
and wild hyacinths were to be found." Let us
cross the meadow, gentle reader, where the path
ran which the Austens must have trod each
Sunday morning as they walked to church.
Leaving the meadow, we enter a small wood,
and, on emerging from this wood, find ourselves
on high tableland. There above us stands the
church, a modest edifice of sober grey, seen
through a screen of great arching elms and sycamores. Behind us stretches a fertile valley fading
into a blue distance. The only sounds that
meet the ear on this still September day are the
twittering of birds and the distant bleating of
sheep. How often must Jane Austen have
listened to these sounds as she passed on her way
to church!

We follow a path which crosses the churchyard
beneath the boughs of an ancient yew-tree, and
enter the small silent church. Our attention is
caught at once by the squire's pew on the right of
the chancel arch. Square and big and towering
above the modern benches it stands—solid oak
below, but with elegant open tracery above through
which the occupants could see and be seen. In
the Austens' time a family named Digweed rented

the Manor of Steventon. Its owner was Mr. Thomas Knight, a distant relative of the Rev. George Austen, but the Digweeds held the property for more than a hundred years.

After examining, with great interest, many tablets to Austens and Digweeds, we quit the dark church and step into the sunshine once more ; and, passing through a wicket gate, find ourselves upon a wide spreading lawn adorned with great sycamores. Beyond the trees rises a stately mansion of early Tudor date, with its stone porch, its heavy mullioned windows, and its great chimney-stacks all wreathed with ivy—the old Manor House of Steventon.

The house is no longer inhabited, for the present owner, we learn, has migrated to a new mansion erected hard by, but the old building itself has suffered no alteration, as far as its outward walls are concerned, since the Digweeds lived there, when there was much intercourse between the squire's and the rector's families.

We sit down upon a grassy bank under the snade of tall limes and, looking to the right of the old grey building, we can see the corner of a gay flower garden, whose red and white dahlias and yellow sunflowers rise above a high box hedge. To our left is a bowling-green, across which the shadows of great trees are sweeping. Whilst my companion sketches the porch of the Manor House

THE OLD MANOR HOUSE

Steventon

I turn over the leaves of Jane Austen's " Letters '
and my eye falls upon these playful remarks,
written in November 1800 to her sister Cassandra :
" The three Digweeds all came on Tuesday, and
we played a pool at commerce. James Digweed
left Hampshire to-day. I think he must be in
love with you, from his anxiety to have you go
to the Faversham balls, and likewise from his
supposing that the two elms fell from their grief at
your absence. Was not it a gallant idea ? It never
occurred to me before, but I daresay it was so."

We are told that " Mr. Austen used to join
Mr. Digweed in buying twenty or thirty sheep,
and that all might be fair it was their custom to
open the pen, and the first half of the sheep which
ran out were counted as belonging to the rector.
Going down to the fold on one occasion after this
process had been gone through, Mr. Austen remarked one sheep among his lot larger and finer
than the rest. ' Well, John,' he observed to John
Bond (his factotum), ' I think we have had the
best of the luck with Mr. Digweed to-day, in
getting that sheep.' ' Maybe not so much in the
luck as you think, sir,' responded the faithful John,
' I see'd her the moment I come in and set eyes on
the sheep, so when we opened the pen I just giv'd
her a " huck " with my stick, and out a' run.' " *

* "Letters of Jane Austen," edited, with an Introduction and
Critical Remarks, by Edward, Lord Brabourne. Macmillan.

Jane Austen

When evening approaches we leave the old manor house and its smooth lawns under the glowing light of the setting sun and descend the hill to Steventon Lane. There our chaise awaits us and we make our way, not back to Deane, but on to Popham Lane, the main road between Basingstoke and Micheldever, and establish ourselves at an old posting inn, called the Wheatsheaf, which we find will be within reach of many a place visited by Jane Austen as well as of Steventon.

CHAPTER III

STEVENTON

*" Love and Joy and friendly Mirth
Bless this roof, these walls, this hearth."*

WE are soon again at Steventon, and now, whilst sketches of the manor house and of the church are progressing, I will glance through my note-books, and endeavour to realise the conditions of life in Steventon Parsonage more than a hundred years ago.

Jane Austen, who, as many of us are aware, was born on December 16, 1775, passed the greater part of her life in Hampshire, first at Steventon and afterwards at Chawton, Just twelve years later than this date, on the same day of the same month, and in the same county, a sister authoress was born. The two writers never met, but we shall find that they frequently cross and recross each other's path—a fortunate circumstance indeed, for the writings of Mary Russell Mitford often describe the surroundings of Jane Austen.

Miss Mitford's grandfather, Dr. Russell, was

Jane Austen

rector of Ashe, near Steventon, and her mother, before her marriage, was acquainted with the Austen family, although Jane herself was then only a child. Mary Russell Mitford's path in literature is much more confined than that of her greater contemporary, but it is pleasant to see that the two writers approached their art in the same spirit and chose the same setting or background for their stories, a background which was familiar to both.

In the opening pages of " Our Village," the author, after dwelling upon the attractions of life in a rural hamlet, remarks : " Even in books I like a confined locality, and so do the critics when they talk of the ' Unities.' Nothing is so tiresome as to be whirled half over Europe at the chariot-wheels of a hero, to go to sleep at Vienna and awaken at Madrid ; it produces a real fatigue, a weariness of spirit. On the other hand, nothing is so delightful as to sit down in a country village in one of Miss Austen's delicious novels, quite sure before we leave it to become intimate with every spot and every person it contains." Miss Mitford loved to write of a small compact community, "a little world of our own" she calls it, " close packed and insulated like ants in an ant-hill, or bees in a hive, or sheep in a fold, or nuns in a convent, or sailors in a ship ; where we know every one, are known to every one, and

authorised to hope that every one feels an interest
in us."

Miss Austen also loved "a confined locality in
books." She writes to a young niece, who had
asked for her advice and criticisms respecting a
novel she was composing: "You are collecting
your people delightfully, getting them exactly
into such a spot as is the delight of my life.
Three or four families in a country village is the
very thing to work on, and I hope you will do a
great deal more, and make full use of them while
they are so favourably arranged."

A third distinguished author, Gilbert White,
born many years earlier than Jane Austen, was
still living and in Hampshire during her girlhood,
and whilst she was learning her lessons he was
recording at Selborne in his letters and diaries
the various occurrences of his "tranquil uneventful
life," told with all "the simple humour of a happy
naturalist."

It is remarkable that these three writers, who
have each left such a powerful mark on the literature of our country, should have been born in the
same county and have been, for some years at
least, contemporaries. And it is also remarkable
that they, who have given to the world works so
full of peace and happiness and racy humour,
should have lived through the tragic period of the
French Revolution. A faint echo of the storm

comes to us occasionally in their *letters*, but their *works* reflect only their own healthful natures and peaceful surroundings.

We must remember, however, that in those days foreign intelligence came slowly and long after the event, and that travelling, which now unites all nations in personal knowledge of each other, was then difficult and expensive. Even at home the movements of country people were much restricted by the condition of the roads. Mr. Austen-Leigh, in his biography of his aunt, tells us that "it was not unusual to set men to work with shovel and pickaxe to fill up ruts and holes" in side roads and lanes "on such special occasions as a funeral or a wedding." The Rev. George Austen kept "a pair of carriage horses," which were necessary in those days "if ladies were to move about at all;" the style of carriage then in vogue being too heavy to be drawn by a single horse over the rough roads. "The horses, probably, like Mr. Bennet's in 'Pride and Prejudice,' were often employed in farm work."

Ladies did not walk much abroad. Their shoes were too thin for such exercise. We remember how Elizabeth Bennet, on first arriving at Hunsford, turned back when Mr. Collins, in the pride of his heart, wished to take her from the inspection of his garden to that of his meadow,

Steventon

"not having shoes to encounter the remains of a white frost." And yet Elizabeth was attired for travelling, having just alighted from a postchaise that had brought her and her friends from London. It is true that in bad weather ladies could walk for a short distance in pattens, which were foot-clogs supported upon an iron ring that raised the wearer a couple of inches from the ground. But these were clumsy contrivances. The rings made a clinking noise on any hard surface, and there is a notice in the vestibule of an old church in Bath, stating that "it is requested by the church-wardens that no persons walk in this church with pattens on."

Many country ladies, however, like Mrs. Primrose, were too much engaged with domesticities to have even time for much walking. Young ladies often assisted in cooking the daintier parts of the family meals. Recipes were handed down from generation to generation. "One house would pride itself on its ham, another on its game-pie, and a third on its superior furmity or tansey-pudding. Beer and home-made wines, especially mead, were largely consumed." Miss Austen remarks in one of her letters : "We hear that there is to be no honey this year. Bad news for us. We must husband our stock of mead. I am sorry to perceive that our stock of twenty gallons is nearly out." Our ancestors must have required some patience in the production of this beverage, for, according to a cookery book, mead, made in the old style, had to stand for fifteen months before it was fit for use; made in the modern style it stands but for half an hour.

Mr. Austen-Leigh feels sure that the ladies of the parsonage house "had nothing to do with the mysteries of the stew-pot or the preserving pan . . . but it is probable," he adds, "that their way of life differed a little from ours, and would have appeared to us more homely." Jane frequently managed the housekeeping for her mother during the absence of her elder sister. Writing to Cassandra in November 1798, she remarks playfully: "My mother desires me to tell you that I am a very good housekeeper, which I have no reluctance in doing, because I really think it my peculiar excellence, and for this reason—I always take care to provide such things as please my own appetite, which I consider as the chief merit in housekeeping."

A frequent visitor at the parsonage was Jane's little niece Anna—the child of her eldest brother James by his first wife who died in 1795. This lady had "been a very tender mother, and the poor little girl missed her so much and kept so constantly asking for 'mama' that her father sent her to Steventon to be taken care of and consoled by her aunts Cassandra and Jane." This 'Anna' has left in manuscript the following description of the house and of its inmates :

"The rectory at Steventon had been of the

STEVENTON PARSONAGE (BACK VIEW)

most miserable description, but in the possession of my grandfather it became a tolerably roomy and convenient habitation; he added and improved, walled in a good kitchen garden, and planted out the east wind, enlarging the house

Jane Austen

until it came to be considered a very comfortable family residence.

"On the sunny side was a shrubbery and flower garden, with a terrace walk of turf which communicated by a small gate with what was termed 'the wood walk,' a path winding through clumps of underwood and overhung by tall elm-trees, skirting the upper side of the home meadows. The lower bow-window, which looked so cheerfully into the sunny garden and up the middle grass walk bordered with strawberries, to the sundial at the end, was that of my grand-father's study, his own exclusive property, safe from the bustle of all household cares.

"The dining, or common sitting-room, looked to the front and was lighted by two casement windows. On the same side the front door opened into a much smaller parlour, and visitors, who were few and rare, were not a bit the less welcome to my grandmother because they found her sitting there busily engaged with her needle, making and mending.

"In later times . . . a sitting-room was made upstairs, 'the dressing-room,' as they were pleased to call it, perhaps because it opened into a smaller chamber in which my two aunts slept. I re-member the common-looking carpet with its chocolate ground, and the painted press with shelves above for books, and Jane's piano, and an oval glass that hung between the windows; but the charm of the room, with its scanty furniture and cheaply-papered walls, must have been, for those old enough to understand it, the flow of native household wit, with all the fun and non-sense of a large and clever family. Here were written the two first of my aunt Jane's completed works, 'Sense and Sensibility' and 'Pride and Prejudice.'"

The same niece writes of her grandfather, the Rev. George Austen: "As a young man I have always understood that he was considered extremely handsome, and it was a beauty which stood by him all his life. At the time when I have the most perfect recollection of him he must have been hard upon seventy, but his hair in its milk-whiteness might have belonged to a much older man. It was very beautiful, with short curls about the ears. His eyes were not large, but of a peculiar and bright hazel. My aunt Jane's were something like them, but none of the children had precisely the same excepting my uncle Henry.

" His wife (Cassandra Leigh) used always to say 'she had never been a beauty,' but that may have been only by comparison with her sister Jane, who married the Rev. Edward Cooper and who was remarkably handsome.

"Cassandra was a little, slight woman, with fine,

Jane Austen

well-cut features, large grey eyes, and good eye-brows, but without any brightness of complexion. She was amusingly particular about people's noses, having a very aristocratic one herself, which she had the pleasure of transmitting to a good many of her children.

" She was a quick-witted woman with plenty of sparkle and spirit in her talk, who could write an excellent letter, either in prose or verse, making no pretence to poetry but being simply playful common sense in rhyme.

" During the early part of her married life her usual dress was a riding-habit made of scarlet cloth, which in due course was cut up into jackets and trousers for her boys."

CHAPTER IV

THE ABBEY SCHOOL

" The ancient monastery's halls,
A solemn pile."

THE same writer, who gives us the description of
Steventon Parsonage and its inhabitants, speaks
of a school at Reading, to which, at an earlier
date, her aunts Cassandra and Jane were sent.
The school adjoined the remains of the ancient
Abbey of Reading, and was called the Abbey
School.   It was kept by a Madame Latournelle,
an Englishwoman, but widow of a Frenchman.

"This school at Reading," writes Miss F. C.
Lefroy,* "was rather a free and easy one judging
by Mrs. Sherwood's† account of it when she was
there some years later (than the Austens), and when
several French *émigrés* were among its masters.
In Cassandra and Jane's days the girls do not
seem to have been kept very strictly, as they and
their cousin, Jane Cooper, were allowed to accept

* A daughter of " Anna's."
† Author of the " Fairchild Family " and other popular tales.

an invitation to dine at an inn with their respective brothers, Edward Austen and Edward
Cooper."

We seem to see the merry faces of the five
young people and to hear their eager chatter as
they sat at table in the old-fashioned inn parlour
enjoying their holiday feast! Jane was very
young at that time, for she was sent to school

A HOLIDAY FEAST

" not because she was thought old enough to
profit much by the instruction there imparted,
but because she would have been miserable (at
home) without her sister ; her mother observing
that ' if Cassandra were going to have her head
cut off, Jane would insist on sharing her fate.' "*

Did the Abbey School, we wonder, serve as a
model for Mrs. Goddard's school in " Emma "?
Mrs. Goddard " was a plain motherly kind of

* ' Memoir," by J. E. Austen-Leigh.

The Abbey School

woman," we are told, whose school was "not a seminary, or an establishment, or anything which professed, in long sentences of refined nonsense, to combine liberal acquirements with elegant morality upon new principles and new systems, and where young ladies, for enormous pay, might be screwed out of health and into vanity; but a real honest old-fashioned boarding-school, where a reasonable quantity of accomplishments were sold at a reasonable price, and where girls might be sent to be out of the way, and scramble themselves into a little education without any danger of coming back prodigies." Mrs. Goddard "had an ample house and garden, gave the children plenty of wholesome food, let them run about a great deal in the summer, and in winter dressed their chilblains with her own hands."

Mrs. Sherwood (then Miss Butt), who went to the Reading school in 1790, a few years after Jane Austen had left it, tells us that "the greater part of the house was encompassed by a beautiful old-fashioned garden, where the young ladies were allowed to wander under tall trees in hot summer evenings." Around two parts of this garden was an artificial embankment, from the top of which, she says, "we looked down upon certain magnificent ruins, as I suppose, of the church begun by Henry I., and consecrated by Becket in 1125." The abbey itself consisted partly of the remains of an ancient building, once the abode of the Benedictine monks, and "the third in size and wealth of all English abbeys," and partly of additions made to the structure in more modern times. Mrs. Sherwood speaks of "an antique gateway with rooms above its arch, and with vast staircases on either side, whose

THE ABBEY GATEWAY AND ABBEY SCHOOL

balustrades had originally been gilt." This gateway "stood without the garden walls, looking upon the Forbury, or open green, which belonged to the town, and where Dr. Valpy's* boys played after school hours." We have been fortunate in discovering an old print of this same "antique gateway," which also shows a part of the school-house itself. Beyond the Forbury there

* Head-master of the Grammar School.

The Abbey School

" rose the tower of the fine old church of Saint Nicholas," while, near at hand, was "the jutting corner of Friar Street" and the "old irregular shops of the market-place."

The abbey, with its past history and its relics of ancient grandeur, must have been a delightful abode to the child Jane Austen, and may it not have suggested to her mind in later life some of the features of "Northanger Abbey"?

Mrs. Sherwood tells us that Mrs. Latournelle "was a person of the old school—a stout person hardly under seventy, but very active, although she had a cork leg. She had never been seen or known to have changed the fashion of her dress. Her white muslin handkerchief was always pinned with the same number of pins, her muslin apron always hung in the same form; she always wore the same short sleeves, cuffs, and ruffles, with a breast bow to answer the bow in her cap, both being flat with two notched ends."

"Mrs. Latournelle received me," she writes, upon her first arrival at school, "in a wainscoted parlour, the wainscot a little tarnished, while the room was hung round with chenille pieces representing tombs and weeping willows. A screen in cloth-work stood in a corner, and there were several miniatures over the lofty mantel-piece."

Mrs. Sherwood describes her sojourn at this school as a "very happy one," remarking that

Jane Austen

"from the ease and liveliness of the mode of life" it "had been particularly delightful" to her. Before she left, the school had passed into the hands of a Monsieur and Madame St. Quintin (the former being a French *émigré*), while Mrs. Latournelle acted chiefly as their housekeeper. A few years later Monsieur and Madame St. Quintin removed to London and started a boarding-school in Hans Place. Thither Miss Mitford went as a pupil in 1798. Many of the traditions of the Reading school were continued in London. Mrs. Sherwood speaks of the theatrical entertainments with which the school terms closed in her day, and possibly these were introduced even earlier. The Austens, as a family, were fond of acting and excelled in it; and though Cassandra and Jane, when they were at school, would have been too young to take the direction of such matters, they would gladly have taken part in them. We read in Miss Mitford's Life: " Before the pupils went home at Easter or Christmas there was either a ballet, when the sides of the school-room were fitted up with bowers, in which the little girls, who had to dance, were seated, and whence they issued at a signal from Monsieur Duval, the dancing-master, attired as sylphs or shepherdesses, to skip or glide through the mazy movements, to the music of his kit; or there was a dramatic performance, as when the same room

The Abbey School

was converted into a theatre for the representation of Hannah More's 'Search after Happiness'; and an elocution-master attended the rehearsals and instructed the actors in their parts."

On one occasion Miss Mitford had to recite the prologue, but before doing this it was considered necessary by the dancing-master that she should perform an elaborate curtsey—a curtsey that should comprehend in its respectful sinking, turning in a semicircle and rising again, the whole audience. This manœuvre was practised at the last dress rehearsal again and again under Monsieur Duval's vociferous instructions, the pupil secretly longing to effect her escape, when suddenly there appeared on the stage the professor of elocution, "a sour pedant of Oxford growth," who denounced the curtsey as ridiculous. Whereupon a scene ensued between the gentlemen much like that in the "Bourgeois Gentilhomme" between the Maître de Philosophie and the Maître de Danse—which happily ended in a verdict that the elaborate curtsey should be abolished and that three short bends of the body should be given in its place.

CHAPTER V

*"'Tis pleasant through the loopholes of retreat
To peep at such a world. . . ."*

HAVING glanced backwards at "the short school course" of Cassandra and Jane we will return with them, in fancy, to Steventon Parsonage.

Let us take a peep into "the common sitting-room with its two casement windows looking to the front;" that is to say commanding a view across the "sweep" and green lawn, to Steventon Lane, and beyond the lane to the grassy slopes of a hill, crowned with wood, that rises on the further side of the shallow valley.

In this sitting-room, as in the other rooms of the parsonage, we are told, "no cornice marked the junction of wall and ceiling, and the great beams, which supported the floor above, projected into the room below, covered only by a coat of paint or whitewash. Carpets were used sparingly in those days even in grand houses. We remember that in describing the "Great House" at

Steventon and the Outer World

"Uppercross" the old-fashioned parlour is spoken of "with a small carpet and shining floor, to which the present daughters of the house were giving the proper air of confusion by a grand piano and a harp." In the Steventon parlour the polished floor would reflect the light from the two casement windows, and those windows would have, probably, curtains hung on runner cords such as Cowper alludes to in the "Task" when he exclaims :

> "Now stir the fire, and close the shutters fast.
> *Let fall* the curtains, wheel the sofa round.
> .   .   .   .   .   .
> So let us welcome peaceful evening in."

Other details we can also imagine—the stiff-backed chairs with carpet-worked seats, the Pembroke table in the centre, like that upon which Mr. Woodhouse had always been accustomed to have his meals ; the fireplace with hobs and high moulded chimney-piece, adorned with miniatures in black frames. Among these miniatures we may fancy the portraits of Jane's two sailor brothers, for these are still in existence. One is a coloured likeness of Francis in the picturesque uniform of a naval officer at the end of the eighteenth century, the other a pencil sketch of Charles as a midshipman. We may also venture to place a tambour frame of polished wood in one corner of the room, for such a frame we know

Jane Austen

Jane used for her delicate embroidery; and we may fancy, perhaps, the best gilt tea-service seen behind the lattice windows of a corner cupboard.

Writing one December evening to Cassandra, who was staying with their brother Edward and his family at Godmersham Park, Jane remarks: "We dine now at half-past three and have done dinner, I suppose, before you begin. We drink tea at half-past six. I am afraid you will despise us. My father reads Cowper to us. How do you spend your evenings?"

Life flowed peacefully and quietly, as a rule, at the parsonage, but every now and then a great whiff of excitement came from the outer world in the shape of letters from the brothers at sea, who were both serving in our great naval wars. To read of their exploits and of their heroism, as recorded in naval histories and biographies, seems to bring us very near to Captain Wentworth, Captain Harville and young William Price.

Francis was a year and a half older than Jane, while Charles, the youngest of the family, was her junior by nearly four years. "Our own particular little brother," she calls him, sometimes, in letters to her sister.

We hear of Charles, as a young midshipman, serving on board the *Unicorn* frigate, under Captain Thomas Williams. Captain Williams had married the Austens' cousin Jane Cooper,

ACTION BETWEEN THE ENGLISH FRIGATE "UNICORN" AND THE FRENCH FRIGATE "LA TRIBUNE," JUNE 8, 1796

who the reader may remember was at the Abbey School with Jane and Cassandra, and who formed one of the party of five young people who dined together at the Reading Inn. The *Unicorn* did battle with many a ship sailing under the enemy's flag, and we read in James's " History of the British Navy," of her taking captive the Dutch brig-of-war *Comet*, the French troopship *La Ville de l'Orient* and the French frigate *La Tribune*. The action with the *Tribune* took place off the Scilly Isles on June 8, 1796. It is represented in the accompanying print, which is taken from a picture, painted in oils upon a wooden panel, now in the possession of a granddaughter of Charles Austen. The picture is supposed to have been painted by one of the officers of the *Unicorn*.

The two ships carried on a running fight we read for ten hours. During this fight the *Unicorn* suffered greatly in sails and rigging, being at one time almost disabled. Twice the *Tribune* attempted to make her escape, under cover of the enveloping smoke, and twice was she pursued by the *Unicorn* till finally that ship getting to close quarters, discharged a " few well-directed broadsides " which brought down the mainmast, mizen and topmast of the *Tribune* and forced her to surrender.

In the meantime, Francis, who from his excellent conduct " was marked out by the Lords of the Admiralty for early promotion," had seen much service in the East Indies and elsewhere. In 1798, he was serving as Senior Lieutenant in various ships on the home station.

Jane writes to her sister Cassandra on December 1 of that year. "I have just heard from Frank. He was at Cadiz alive and well on October 19, and had then very lately received a letter from you, written as long ago as when the *London* was at St. Heliers. Lord St. Vincent had left the fleet when he wrote, and was gone to Gibraltar.

"Frank writes in good spirits, but says that our correspondence cannot be so easily carried on in future, as it has been, as the communication between Cadiz and Lisbon is less frequent than formerly. You and my mother, therefore, must not alarm yourselves at the long intervals that may divide his letters. I address this advice to you two as being the most tender-hearted of the family."

A little later she writes : " I have got some pleasant news for you which I am eager to communicate.

"Admiral Gambier, in reply to my father's application, writes as follows : 'With regard to your son now in the *London*, I am glad I can give you the assurance that his promotion is likely to take place very soon, as Lord Spencer has been so

good as to say he would include him in an arrangement that he proposes making in a short time
relative to some promotion in that quarter.'

"There! I may now finish my letter and go and
hang myself, for I am sure I can neither write,
nor do, anything which will not appear insipid to
you after this."

A month later Jane writes, joyfully, "Frank is
made! He was yesterday raised to the rank of
commander and appointed to the *Petterel* sloop,
now at Gibraltar. A letter from Daysh has just
announced this, and as it is confirmed by a very
friendly one from Mr. Mathew to the same effect,
transcribing one from Admiral Gambier to the
general, we have no reason to suspect the truth
of it." *

Does not this remind us of the letters announcing young William Price's promotion, when
it appeared from the secretary's note that the
first lord "had the very great happiness of attending to the recommendation of Sir Charles;
that Sir Charles was much delighted in having
such an opportunity of proving his regard for
Admiral Crawford, and that the circumstance of
Mr. William Price's commission being made out
was spreading general joy through a wide circle
of great people?"

Jane continues: "As soon as you have cried a

* "Letters," Lord Brabourne.

little for joy, you may go on, and learn farther . . . that Lieutenant Charles John Austen is removed to the *Tamar* frigate—this comes from the admiral.

" This letter is to be dedicated entirely to good news. If you will send my father an account of your expenses he will send you a draft for the amount. If you don't buy a muslin gown on the strength of this money and Frank's promotion I shall never forgive you." *

The *Petterel*, we learn from naval records, was a sloop of twenty-four guns and one hundred and twenty men. In the June following his assuming her command, Francis Austen "participated in Lord Keith's capture of a French squadron under Rear-Admiral Perrée," and early in the year 1800 " he greatly signalised himself in an encounter off Marseilles with three French vessels, two of which he drove on to the rocks and the third he captured. All this was accomplished without the loss of a man to the *Petterel*, although thirty of her crew, together with the first lieutenant and gunners, were absent." The ship captured was the *Ligurienne*, " a fine vessel of her class and in excellent repair. She was built in a very peculiar manner, being fastened throughout with screw-bolts, so that she might be taken to pieces and set up again with ease. She was originally intended, so

* " Letters," Lord Brabourne.

said the French prisoners, to follow Buonapart to Egypt."

A few months later the *Petterel* formed part of the squadron of Sir Sydney Smith off the coast of Egypt. Whilst there Captain Austen, by a gallant action, prevented a Turkish line of battle-ship, of eighty guns, from falling into the hands of the French. The ship had been wrecked near to the Island of Aboukir and was totally dismantled. Already three hundred of the enemy had commenced their work of plunder when they were driven off and their prize set on fire ; while thirteen men, the remainder of the Greek crew, were saved.

Charles Austen joined his new ship the *Tamar* in February 1799, but he was shortly afterwards reappointed to the *Endymion*. In this frigate, commanded by Sir Thomas Williams, his former captain of the *Unicorn*, "he came into frequent contact with the enemy's gun-boats off the southern coast of Spain and assisted in making prizes of several privateers. On the occasion of the capture of the *Scipio*, of eighteen guns and one hundred and forty men, which surrendered during a violent gale, he very intrepidly put off in a boat with only four men, and having boarded the vessel, succeeded in retaining possession of her until the following day," when he handed her over to his captain.

Jane Austen

Jane writes to her sister: "Charles has received £30 for his share in the privateer, and expects £10 more; but of what avail is it to take prizes if he lays out the produce in presents to his sisters? He has been buying gold chains and topaz crosses for us. He must be well scolded."*

Great were the rejoicings at the parsonage when either of the sailor brothers returned home for a flying visit. We hear of Charles accompanying his sister Jane to the balls of the neighbourhood and of his being "very much admired," and being considered by one friend as "handsomer than Henry." Charles in the meantime enjoyed the gaiety fully as much as William Price enjoyed the famous ball at Mansfield Park, and probably he and his partner were often among "the five or six determined couples who were still hard at work" at a late hour, when others, like Fanny, had to retire to rest.

Henry, Jane's third brother, is thus described by his niece, the "Anna" whose writings we have already quoted. "He was the handsomest of the family, and, in the opinion of his own father, the most talented. There were others who formed a different estimate, but, for the most part, he was greatly admired. Brilliant in conversation he was, and, like his father, blessed with a hopefulness of temper which, in adapting itself to all

* "Letters," Lord Brabourne.

48

THE REV. GEORGE AUSTEN PRESENTING HIS SON EDWARD TO MR. AND MRS. THOMAS KNIGHT

Steventon and the Outer World

circumstances, even the most adverse, served to create a perpetual sunshine." That Jane delighted in his society is evident by her letters.

Out of all her five brothers one only was settled within reach of Steventon, namely James, the eldest of the family. Mrs. George Austen said of this son that "he possessed in the highest degree, classical knowledge, literary taste, and the power of elegant composition." Being ten years older than Jane, it is believed that he had "a large share in directing her reading and forming her taste." After a career at college, James took Holy Orders, and, at the time we are writing of, had become vicar of Sherborne St. John's; but he also acted as resident curate for his father at Deane. He was twice married. His first wife (the mother of "Anna") being a daughter of General Mathew, the Governor of New Granada. She died suddenly in 1795, and James took for his second wife a Miss Lloyd, a member of a family with whom the Austens were intimate.

Edward, Jane's second brother, had been adopted, when a child, by his cousin, Mr. Thomas Knight, of Godmersham Park in Kent and of Chawton House in Hampshire. Mr. Knight had no children of his own, and Edward Austen eventually assumed his name after inheriting his estates. The event of the boy being handed over to the Knight family is commemorated in a curious

silhouette group which hangs in Chawton House.
Mrs. Knight is represented as seated at a small table
playing at chess with a lady friend, whilst Mr.
Knight, who has been watching the game, stands
behind her chair. Mr. Austen is in the act of presenting his son, and the child—a comical little
figure in a tight-fitting coat and knee-breeches—
stretches out his hands towards his adopted
parents.

Although Edward was thus removed from home
early in ife, a strong tie of affection bound him and
his family together. After his marriage we find
his sisters, in turn, frequently visiting him first at
Rowling, a small property in East Kent, belonging to the Bridges family, and afterwards at Godmersham Park, and Jane's letters, either to or
from these places, show what a lively interest she
took in all that concerned both him and his. His
wife—the " Elizabeth " of the letters—was a
daughter of Sir Brook Bridges, of Goodnestone
in Kent. Mr. Knight died in 1794, and his widow
generously insisted upon handing over the property to Edward,* and retired to a house called
"White Friars" in Canterbury. There Jane
occasionally visited her.

* Some interesting letters written on this occasion are given in
Mr. Walter Pollock's book, entitled " Jane Austen, her Contemporaries and her Critics," which appeared in 1899.

CHAPTER VI

THE COUNTY BALL-ROOM

" On with the dance ! let joy be unconfined."

Miss Jane Austen dearly loved a ball. Who can doubt this who has read the various descriptions of balls in her novels—all full, as they are, of life and movement and racy humour, while each one is perfectly distinct in character ?

Frequent allusions are made in the " Letters ' to the county balls at Basingstoke. These took place, it seems, once a month on a Thursday during the season. They were held in the Assembly Rooms, and were frequented by all the well-to-do families of the out-lying neighbour-hood ; many of them, like the Austens, coming from long distances, undeterred by the dangers of dark winter nights, lampless lanes, and stormy weather.

Now, where could those Assembly Rooms have been situated ? Guide-books were silent on the subject ; but probably they formed part of the chief inn of Basingstoke. We learnt from the country people that the old " Angel," standing in the market-place, was, in former times, the principal inn and posting-house.

With a firm determination to discover the county ball-room or, at least, the place where it stood, we set off for Basingstoke on a bright September morning. Having crossed the busy market-place we drew up in front of the " Angel," with its tiled roof and white window frames. The upper part of the building is evidently unchanged, but shop-windows occupy the ground floor where the stage-coaches formerly rolled through a wide entrance to the yard beyond. The West of England coaches, we are told, used to halt here for their passengers to dine, bringing for one short hour a whirl of excitement and bustle into the quiet sleepy town.

The house is still a place for refreshment, so we entered and made inquiries as to its former condition. The master, in reply, produced an old bill-head with a view of the inn upon it. We noticed, over the coach-entrance, a carved wooden lintel. "See, there it is, ma'am," he remarked, pointing to the lintel, which hung from a beam across the ceiling. We now questioned him about the Assembly Rooms, but here he was unable to help us, not knowing anything about them. So, after taking some lunch, we were regretfully pre·paring to depart when, by chance, we fell in with

The County Ball-room

the wife of our host. Prepared for disappointment we put the same questions to her, but now there came to us a sudden ray of light and leading. She told us that beyond the old stables and coach-houses at the back of the inn, there was a large room, now used as a hay-loft, but which, she had been told, was once a ball-room. In old times it was connected with the inn by a long passage, that ran above the stables and harness-rooms, but now the only access to it was from the great coaching-yard. Should we like to see the loft? The owner of it, and of all the out-buildings was a horse-dealer, who she was sure would permit us to do so, and she would, herself, show us the way.

And so, following our guide, we step into a paved covered way, and, passing the long low mangers where the post-horses fed, come out into the coaching-yard. There on the left stand the buildings described. We mount some wooden steps leading to the so-called hay-loft, and in another moment we find ourselves in the old Assembly Room! Piles of hay cover the floor, but we cannot mistake the place. There are the handsome chimney-pieces, the sash windows and the double-flap doors that mark a reception-room of importance; and when we push aside the litter beneath our feet, the fine even planking of a dancing-floor appears. As we gaze around us,

Jane Austen

the discoloured and mouldering plaster on the walls, the broken panes, the cobweb festoons, the forlorn and rusty grates, and the piles of hay all vanish, and we seem to see the room as it appeared in its palmy days when prepared for a county ball. A chandelier, resplendent with wax candles, hangs in the middle of the room. Its

THE COUNTY BALL-ROOM

lights are reflected in the polished floor beneath and again in the oval mirrors above the two chimney-pieces. Fires are blazing in the hearths. See, there are the musicians, in their tie-wigs and knee-breeches, just entering, and soon the gay company will be arriving. Amidst that gay company there is one figure around which all the interest of the past is gathered. Let us glance for a moment at Miss Jane Austen as she enters the ball-room.

The County Ball-room

She is rather tall, is slender, and remarkably graceful. "Her step is light and firm, and her whole appearance expressive of health and animation." In complexion she is "a clear brunette, with a rich colour, hazel eyes, fine features, and curling brown hair." Resembling, in fact, her own Emma Woodhouse, as described by Mrs. Weston when she exclaims: "Such an eye!—the true hazel eye—and so brilliant! regular features, open countenance, with a complexion—oh what a bloom of full health, and such a pretty height and size, such a firm and upright figure."

And as to her attire, we may fancy Jane wearing a soft white muslin gown with a frill at the bottom just falling to her ancles in front and forming a small train behind; "a bit of the same muslin" round her head, confined by a narrow band of ribbon or velvet, and surmounted by "one little comb"; "green shoes" on her feet and "a white fan" in her hand.

Writing to her sister during the Christmas of 1798, of a ball that had just taken place in the Assembly Rooms, she says: "There were thirty-one people, and only eleven ladies out of the number. Of the gentlemen present you may have some idea from the list of my partners: Mr. Wood, G. Lefroy, Rice, a Mr. Butcher, Mr. Temple, Mr. William Orde, Mr. John Harwood, and Mr. Calland, who appeared, as usual, with his hat in

Jane Austen

his hand, and stood every now and then behind Catherine and me to be talked to and abused for not dancing. We teased him, however, into it at last. I was very glad to see him again after so long a separation, and he was altogether rather the genius and flirt of the evening." * Did this Mr. Calland, we wonder, suggest some of the traits of the inimitable Tom Musgrave?

The "Catharine" alluded to was a Miss Catherine Bigg, a daughter of Mr. Bigg Wither, of Manydown Park. This gentleman had assumed the name of Wither on inheriting the estate. Manydown is within easy reach of Basingstoke, and Jane often stayed there when the Assembly balls took place. She had done so on the present occasion.

Writing of another dance, in the Assembly Rooms, Jane remarks : " It was a pleasant ball, and still more good than pleasant, for there were nearly sixty people, and sometimes we had seventeen couples. The Portsmouths, Dorchesters, Boltons, Portals and Clerks were there, and all the meaner and more usual etcs. There was a scarcity of men in general. I danced nine dances out of ten—five with Stephen Terry, T. Chute, and James Digweed, and four with Catherine. There was commonly a couple of ladies standing up together." *

* " Letters," Lord Brabourne.

The County Ball-room

When the grand people mentioned above entered the room, we can imagine the same sort of commotion occurring as is described in " The Watsons." " After some minutes of extraordinary bustle without, and watchful curiosity within, the important party, preceded by the attentive master of the inn, to open a door which was never shut, made their appearance." In the present case the master of the inn, we find, was a man named Curtis ; his family having managed the " Angel " for two generations. He was a clever huntsman, and is mentioned with praise in the " Vine Hunt."

A propos of another ball at the " Rooms," Jane says : " There were more dancers than the room could hold, which is enough to constitute a good ball at any time. I do not think I was very much in request. People were rather apt not to ask me till they could not help it. There was one gentleman, an officer of the Cheshire, a very good-looking young man, who, I was told, wanted very much to be introduced to me ; but as he did not want it quite enough to take much trouble in effecting it, we never could bring it about." And again she writes : " Our ball was chiefly made up of Jervoises and Terrys. I had an odd set of partners ; Mr. Jenkins, Mr. Street, Colonel Jervoise, James Digweed, J. Lyford and Mr. Briggs, a friend of the latter. I had a very pleasant evening, however, though you will probably find out that there was no particular reason for it; but I do not think it worth while to wait for enjoyment until there is some real opportunity for it." *

Balls in the days of Miss Austen consisted mainly of country dances, for the stately minuet was going out of vogue, while the rapid waltz had not yet come in. We must picture to ourselves the ladies and gentlemen ranged in two long rows facing one another, whilst the couples at the extreme ends danced down the set; the most important lady present having been privileged to " call " or lead off the dance. We remember how Emma Woodhouse had to give way, on such an occasion, to the right of Mrs. Elton, as a bride, to lead.

Jane excelled greatly in the dance, and she shared her own Elizabeth Bennet's dislike of an incompetent partner. In one of her letters she speaks of sitting down during two dances in preference to having to stand up with a gentleman " who danced too ill to be endured." Was he, we wonder, like Mr. Collins, " awkward and solemn, apologising instead of attending, and often moving wrong without being aware of it ? "

A good partner for a country dance was a matter of consequence as the engagement, implying, as it did, two dances, occupied a large part of the evening. We remember Henry Tilney's

* " Letters," Lord Brabourne.

The County Ball-room

playful remarks on the subject to Catherine Morland when their intercourse had been interrupted for a few minutes by the irrepressible John Thorpe. "He has no business to withdraw the attention of my partner from me. We have entered into a contract of mutual agreeableness for the space of an evening, and all our agreeableness belongs solely to each other for that time. I consider a country dance as an emblem of marriage. Fidelity and complaisance are the principal duties of both ; and those men who do not choose to dance or marry themselves, have no business with the partners or wives of their neighbours."

When the dance was over we may fancy the company repairing to the large front parlour of the "Angel" for supper. They would traverse the long passage, already mentioned, to do so. Did it, we wonder, suggest to our authoress, the long passage at the "Crown," when, "supper being announced, the move began ; and Miss Bates might be heard from that moment without interruption, till her being seated at table and taking up her spoon. 'Jane, Jane, my dear Jane where are you? Here is your tippet, Mrs. Weston begs you to put on your tippet. She says she is afraid there will be draughts in the passage, though everything has been done—one door nailed up—quantities of matting—my dear Jane, indeed you must. Mr. Churchill oh ! you are too

Jane Austen

obliging! How well you put it on!—so gratified!
. . . Upon my word, Jane on one arm, and me
on the other. . . . Well here we are at the passage.
Two steps, Jane, take care of the two steps. Oh!
no, there is but one. Well I was persuaded there
were two. How very odd! I was convinced
there were two, and there is but one. I never
saw anything equal to the comfort and style—
candles everywhere.'"

We can fancy the lively scene at supper with
its accompaniment of "toasts" patriotic and
private and the proposal of *sentiments*, in accordance with the custom of the day. Perhaps one of
these last might take the form of words used, to
the present writer's knowledge, on a similar
occasion: "May courtship be ever in fashion and
kissing the pink of the mode."

And now the time having arrived for the company to disperse we may think of them driving
along the moonlit highways or narrow lanes of
the neighbourhood on their various homeward
journeys. Let us follow the coach that bears
Miss Jane Austen and Miss Catherine Bigg to
Manydown Park. We think we see them turn
from the main western road to climb the long
grassy slopes of the open park, and then, passing
beneath an avenue of gnarled oaks, come out in
full view of the fine old mansion of Manydown,
with its great sweeping cedar beside it; perhaps,

MANYDOWN PARK

The County Ball-room

at that time, all sparkling with frost or a light fall of snow. Leaving this wintry scene, the two girls enter the hall, cheerful with lights, and ascending the broad staircase with its balustrade of delicate ironwork, are welcomed by the master of the house who has sat up to receive them in the long drawing-room whose three windows, at the further end, form a large bay. Perhaps, as they recount the events of the ball, standing round a blazing fire beneath its carved marble chimney-piece, Jane may be imagined to exclaim with one of her own heroines, " How soon it is at an end! I wish it could all come over again!"

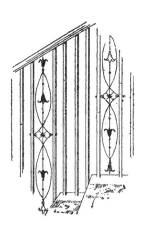

CHAPTER VII

FRIENDS AND NEIGHBOURS

" . . . music, mirth, and social cheer
Speed on their wings the passing year."

AMONG her partners at the Assembly balls Jane
Austen mentions, as we have seen, Stephen
Terry, T. Chute, James Digweed, John Harwood
and J. Lyford.

Stephen Terry belonged to the family of the
Terrys of Dummer, a quaint little village lying
near to Popham Lane and within reach of Steventon. We have visited the village and seen the
squire's mansion where the Terrys lived. It is
a long white house with flat, arched windows and
a square-columned porch, standing a little back
from Dummer Lane. Hard by is the village
church, a very small edifice in comparison with
the squire's mansion. It has a low wooden tower
and a deep tiled roof. On the southern side of
the roof there projects a queer little dormer
window which gives light to a gallery that occupies
the greater part of the interior of the church.

Friends and Neighbours

Here, probably, the squires and their families used to sit. This little church is associated with the name of George Whitefield; for, when quite a young man, he was given the curacy of Dummer. He suffered, at first, from the solitude and silence of the tiny village, and remarks, in a letter, that he "mourned like a dove" for his Oxford friends.

J. Lyford was a grandson of old Dr. Lyford, the chief medical man of Basingstoke. Mr. Austen-Leigh writes of the latter: "I remember him a fine old man, with such a flaxen wig as is not to be seen, or conceived, by this generation. This wig he used to 'dispart with biennially' (as Sir Walter Scott expresses it) and to bestow the reversion of it every second year on an old man in our parish (of Steventon) as tall and fine-looking as himself, producing thereby a ludicrous resemblance between the peasant and the doctor." *

T. Chute belonged to the family of Mr. William Chute who was a prominent figure in the Hampshire society of Miss Austen's day. He was M.P. for the county in the Tory interest, was the owner of the "Vine," and at the head of the Vine Hunt. Mr. Chute seems to have had a singularly amiable, original and humorous disposition. Mr. Austen-Leigh, writing of his boyish

* See "The Vine Hunt," by J. E. Austen-Leigh. (Printed for private circulation.)

recollections of him, says : " He had a fair round face with a most agreeable countenance expressive of good humour and intelligence. . . . I can fancy that I see him, trotting up to the meet at Freefolk Wood, or St. John's, sitting rather loose on his horse, and his clothes rather loose upon him—the scarlet coat flapping open, a little whitened at the collar by the contact of his hair powder and the friction of his pigtail ; the frill of his shirt above, and his gold watch-chain and seal below, both rather prominent, the short knee-breeches scarcely meeting the boot-tops. See ! he rides up ; probably with some original amusing remark, at any rate with a cheerful greeting to his friends, a nod and kindly word to the farmers, and some laughing notice of the schoolboy on his pony.

" Or I could give quite another picture of him in his parish church—standing upright, tilting his heavy folio prayer-book on the edge of his high pew so that he had to look *up* rather than *down* on it. There he stands, like Sir Roger de Coverley, giving out the responses in an audible tone, with an occasional glance to see what tenants were at church, and what school children were misbehaving ; and, sometimes, when the rustic psalmody began its discord in the gallery, with a humour, which even church could not restrain, making some significant gesture to provoke a

smile from me and the other young persons in
the pew."

The same writer gives us some of Mr. Chute s
repartees. "Sir John Cope, who professed Radical
politics, once wrote to him that he had a litter of
five dogs in that year's entry, whose names had
all *pretty much the same meaning*, for they
were Placeman, Parson, Pensioner, Pilferer, and
Plunderer. But the Tory squire, with ready invention, retorted that he would show him a litter
of which the five names were equally synony-
mous, being Radical, Rebel, Regicide, Ruffian,
and Rascal."

Miss Austen has mentioned "the Portals" as
being present at the Assembly balls. There
were two brothers of that name, Mr. William
Portal of Laverstoke House, and Mr. John
Portal of Freefolk Priors—both owning large
landed property. They belonged to the Hugue-
not family of de Portal who fled from France on
the revocation of the Edict of Nantes. Henri,
the ancestor of the Hampshire Portals, who was
a child at the time, was protected by a faithful
nurse and escaped from Bordeaux concealed in a
wine cask, placed on board a fishing boat. He
reached Southampton, where many of the French
refugees were employed in the art of paper-
making. Later on he, himself, established the
paper-mill at Laverstoke, and in 1724 obtained

from the Bank of England that privilege of manufacturing their note-paper which is still held by his descendants of the fourth generation.

We have visited Laverstoke Park, which lies on undulating ground between Overton and Whitchurch. Its magnificent trees have been planted by many generations of Portals. The little river Test runs through the park, a clear and rapid trout stream.

Mr. John Harwood was one of the Harwoods of Deane, " an old family with some racy peculiarities of character. It has been supposed that Fielding took the idea of his Squire Western from the John Harwood of his day; and as Fielding used to visit at Oakley Hall it is not improbable that some features of his immortal Tory Squire might have been copied from this original."*

The old Manor House of Deane, the home of the Harwoods, has already been spoken of. It is built of dark red brick and has white window frames and a white porch. Deane Lane divides its beautiful grounds from those of the old rectory which formerly stood at a little distance behind a thatched mud wall. The mud wall is still standing and behind it lies a sunny fruit and flower garden, but the old rectory, the home for seven years of Mr. and Mrs. George Austen, has long since

* " The Vine Hunt."

disappeared. At the time we are writing of, it was inhabited by Jane Austen's eldest brother James and his family.

Early in January 1796, a ball was given at Deane House, which Jane describes in a letter to her sister. We have seen the room where the dancing must have taken place. Its walls are

DEANE HOUSE

panelled and painted white and it has a grand Jacobean chimney-piece which reaches to the ceiling. The floor is of polished wood. Two windows, deeply recessed in the thickness of the wall, look out on to the park with its waving trees.

At the " Harwood's ball " Jane was somewhat in the position of her own Catherine Morland at the Cotillion ball in Bath, desirous to escape from one gentleman and to be free to dance with another. "To my inexpressible astonishment," she writes, "I entirely escaped

THE PANELLED ROOM IN DEANE HOUSE

John Lyford. I was forced to fight hard for it, however." Was John Lyford, we wonder, borne away from Jane, as his namesake was borne away from Catherine, "by the resistless pressure of a long string of passing ladies"?

Friends and Neighbours

The attractive gentleman on this occasion was a Mr. Tom Lefroy, a nephew of the Rector of Ashe.

"I am almost afraid to tell you," Jane continues, "how my Irish friend and I behaved. Imagine to yourself everything most profligate and shocking in the way of dancing and sitting down together. I *can* expose myself, however, only *once more* because he leaves the country soon after next Friday, on which day we are to have a dance at Ashe. He is a very gentlemanlike, good-looking, pleasant young man I assure you. But as to our having ever met, except at the three last balls, I cannot say much ; for he is so excessively laughed at about me at Ashe that he is ashamed of coming to Steventon." But Jane winds up her letter by saying : "After I had written the above we received a visit from Mr. Tom Lefroy and his cousin George. The latter is really very well behaved now ; and as for the other, he has but one fault, which time will, I trust, entirely remove— it is that his morning coat is a great deal too light. He is a very great admirer of Tom Jones, and therefore wears the same coloured clothes, I imagine, which he did, when he was wounded." Writing a few days later she remarks : "Our party at Ashe to-morrow night will consist of Edward Cooper, James (for a ball is nothing without *him*), Buller, who is now staying with us,

Jane Austen

and I. I look forward with great impatience to
it, as I rather expect to receive an offer from my
friend in the course of the evening. I shall
refuse him, however, unless he promises to give
away his white coat." On the day of the ball she
writes : " At length the day has come on which I
am to flirt my last with Tom Lefroy, and when
you receive this it will be over. My tears flow as
I write at the melancholy idea." *

Now where was the ball-room in which Mr. Tom
Lefroy and Miss Jane Austen talked and laughed
and danced together that last time ? " Ashe," in
Jane's letters, means either Ashe Park (which
belonged to a member of the Portal family) or
Ashe Rectory ; but more frequently it means the
latter, for there was much intercourse between the
Austens and the Lefroys, and this ball was evidently
given by Mr. Tom Lefroy's uncle, the Rev. Isaac
Peter George Lefroy, as a farewell festivity to
the nephew previous to his departure for Ireland.

We must ask the reader to accompany us
in a pilgrimage to Ashe to see, if possible, this
same ball-room. Crossing the fields that lie
between Deane and Ashe, we enter the narrow
lane where the small church stands, and by the
kindness of the present rector, gain admission to
his house, much of which remains as it was in
the days of the Lefroys.

* " Letters," Lord Brabourne.

Friends and Neighbours

Here, in the older part, is the morning-room, which has two casement windows opening on to gay flower-beds and a green lawn, flanked on the side of the lane by a great yew hedge that is nearly as tall as the house itself. In this room

ASHE RECTORY

there are folding doors which open into a large dining-room, which was formerly the drawing-room. "Those doors," remarks the Rector, "were thrown open when the Rev. Isaac Peter George Lefroy gave dances here a hundred years ago.' So we are actually standing on the very spot where the ball took place, and can picture to ourselves the whole scene! There the country dance must have been formed, and there down the centre must Jane and her partner have crossed hands to the couple at the lower end! The pleasant echoes of their merry talk seem hardly to have died away, though the authors of it have so long since vanished.

We hear no more of Mr. Tom Lefroy in the letters, for he and Jane never met again. He became, in after years, Lord Chief Justice of Ireland, and survived Jane by more than half a century, but "even in extreme old age" we are told "he would speak of his former companion as one to be much admired and not easily forgotten by those who had ever known her."*

Many a happy hour must Miss Jane Austen have passed in this house; for the rector's wife, though considerably older than herself, was her intimate friend. "Mrs. Lefroy," we are told, "was a remarkable person. Her rare endowments of goodness, talents, graceful person and engaging manners were sufficient to secure her a prominent place in any society into which she was thrown, while her enthusiastic eagerness of disposition rendered her especially attractive to a clever and lively girl."† "She was," writes her brother, Sir Egerton Brydges, "one of the most amiable and

* "Memoir," by J. E. Austen-Leigh.   † *Ibid.*

Friends and Neighbours

eloquent women I ever knew, and was universally beloved and admired." Even the villagers of Ashe felt the influence of her rare qualities as distinguishing her from other people, and always called her " Madame Lefroy." To Jane such a friend must have been invaluable, but alas! she had the grief of losing her early in 1804, when Mrs. Lefroy was killed by a fall from her horse. The exact spot where the accident took place has been pointed out to us. It is where the narrow lane from Polehampton crosses the Overton Road. Jane wrote some verses in memory of her friend which are given in the " Memoir." They testify the deepest love and admiration and prove how keenly Jane mourned her loss.

We find mention of much friendly visiting among the various neighbours in the " Letters." " On Thursday we walked to Deane," Jane writes in October 1800; " yesterday to Oakley Hall and Oakley, and to-day to Deane again. At Oakley we did a great deal—ate some sandwiches all over mustard, admired Mr. Bramston's porter, and Mrs. Bramston's transparencies, and gained a promise from the latter of two roots of heartsease, one all yellow, the other all purple, for you." A month later she writes : "We had a very pleasant day on Monday at Ashe (Park). We sat down fourteen to dinner in the study, the dining-room being not habitable from the storms having blown down its chimney. There was a whist and a casino table, and six outsiders. Rice and Lucy made love, Mat. Robinson fell asleep, James and Mrs. Augusta alternately read Dr. Finnis' pamphlet on the cow-pox, and I bestowed my company, by turns, on all."

Does not this remind us of some of the evenings at Netherfield, when Elizabeth standing by watched the others playing at cards ; or when Miss Bingley "having obtained private intelligence that Mr. Darcy did not wish for cards," refused Mr. Hurst's petition for them, so that that gentleman had nothing to do but to stretch himself on one of the sofas and go to sleep ; whilst Bingley, in the meantime, lavished his attentions upon Jane Bennet and "talked scarcely to any one else "?

In another letter to Cassandra, Jane remarks playfully : " Your unfortunate sister was betrayed last Thursday into a situation of the utmost cruelty. I arrived at Ashe Park before the party from Deane and was shut up in the drawing-room with Mr. Holder * alone for ten minutes. I had some thoughts of insisting on the housekeeper being sent for, and nothing could prevail on me to move two steps from the door, on the lock of which I kept one hand constantly fixed. We met nobody but ourselves, played at vingt-un again, and were very cross. . . .

* A single middle-aged gentleman with a West Indian fortune who was then renting Ashe Park.

Friends and Neighbours

"You express so little anxiety about my being murdered under Ashe Copse by Mrs. Hulbert's servant, that I have a great mind not to tell you whether I was or not, and shall only say that I did not return home that night or the next. . . . On Friday I wound up my four days of dissipation by meeting William Digweed at Deane, and am pretty well, I thank you, after it."*

We hear, in one of the letters, of a ball to be given by Lady Dorchester at Kempshott House, on January 8, 1799. Lord Dorchester, the husband of this lady, was a military officer of great courage and skill, " who had distinguished himself in the American war," as Sir Guy Carleton. On the conclusion of the war he had been made Governor-General of Quebec, New Brunswick and Nova Scotia, and had been raised to the peerage.

At the time of the projected ball Miss Jane Austen was expecting her youngest brother at Steventon for a flying visit. She writes to her sister on the morning of January 8 : "Charles is not come yet, but he must come this morning or he shall never know what I will do to him. The ball at Kempshott is this evening and I have got him an invitation. . . . I am not to wear my white satin cap to-night, after all ; I am to wear a mamalouc cap instead which Charles Fowle sent to Mary † and which she lends me. It is all the

* "Letters," Lord Brabourne.   † Mrs. James Austen.

75

fashion now; worn at the opera and by Lady Mildmays at Hackwood balls. I hate describing such things and I daresay you will be able to guess what it is like."

The word *Mamalouc* is given as *Mamalone* in Lord Brabourne's "Letters of Jane Austen," which is evidently a clerical error; the letters *uc* in the MS. having been mistaken for *ne*. The battle of the Nile, fought in the preceding August, had set the fashion in ladies' dress for everything suggestive of Egypt and of the hero of Aboukir. In the fashion-plates of the day we find Mamalouc cloaks and Mamalouc robes of flowing red cloth. Ladies wear toupées, somewhat resembling a fez, which we recognise as the "Mamalouc cap." Their hats are adorned with the "Nelson rose feather," and their dainty feet encased in "green morocco slippers bound with yellow and laced with crocodile-coloured ribbon."

Kempshott House lies between Dummer and Popham Lane. Would the owners, we wondered, permit us to see the room in which the ball took place? Inspired by this idea, and by the daring of explorers, we entered Kempshott Park and drove up the long, gentle ascent that leads to the house.

We found it to be a stone classical structure such as Miss Austen describes as "a modern residence." It has a large bowed centre, three

Friends and Neighbours

windows wide, supported by a colonnade of pillars. To our petition for admittance came a friendly rejoinder from the lady of the house, who was soon herself conducting us from room to room, explaining the various alterations effected in later years, and pointing out the parts that are still unchanged. The present drawing-room, it seems, forms a part of the former ball-room.

The house stands on the slope of a hill, and is so built that there is one storey less at the back than at the front. In former times the main entrance was at the back, and there the carriages must have set down the gay company for the ball.

Lord Dorchester took over Kempshott House, in the year 1796, from George, Prince of Wales, who had used it as a hunting residence. At the time of the French Revolution, a large number of *émigrés* of high rank were entertained at Kempshott. On one occasion a grand stag-hunt was got up for their amusement, at which about five hundred horsemen were present. The foreigners were equipped, according to the French mode, with long twisted horns over their shoulders, and their grotesque appearance, it is said, much astounded the Hampshire farmers.*

We hear no particulars of the Kempshott ball, for Jane, writing to her sister on the following

* See " Sporting Reminiscences," by Æsop.

day, complains of a temporary weakness in one of her eyes which makes writing troublesome, adding : " My mother has undertaken to do it for me, and I shall leave the Kempshott ball for her." Many of Mrs. Austen's letters have been preserved, but unluckily this particular one seems to have been lost.

CHAPTER VIII

SCENES OF EARLY WRITINGS

" . . . Friends
Attun'd to happy unison of soul."

THERE are some old copy-books in the possession of the Austen family, containing the first efforts at story-making of the future novelist—then a girl between fourteen and sixteen years of age. These tales are chiefly burlesques, related in mock heroic language, to ridicule the impossible events and highflown sentiments she had met with in various silly romances. The youthful author seems as if she were studying how *not* to write before striking out any path for herself. She manifests her judgment of the "silly romances," "not by direct censure but by the indirect method of imitating and exaggerating the faults of her models, thus clearing the fountain by first stirring up the mud." *

The present writer has read one of these early tales. Its fun is so spontaneous and so irresistibly

_____
* Article upon her works by Lord Acton.

comic that, whilst reading it, one seems almost to hear the merry laugh of the young girl over her own performance.

This style of gentle burlesque never lost its attraction for Miss Austen. We meet with it in many a page of her correspondence as well as in the novels. In " Northanger Abbey " she tells us that Catherine Morland had actually "reached the age of seventeen without having seen one amiable youth who could call forth her sensibility. . . . This was strange indeed. But . . . there was not one lord in the neighbourhood ; no, not even a baronet. There was not one family among their acquaintance who had reared and supported a boy accidentally found at their door ; not one young man whose origin was unknown."

In one of her letters she writes : " Mr. C's opinion is gone down in my list. I will redeem my credit with him by writing a close imitation of ' Self Control ' as soon as I can. I will improve upon it. My heroine shall not only be wafted down an American river in a boat by herself. She shall cross the Atlantic in the same way, and never stop till she reaches Gravesend." How Jane must have enjoyed drawing up her "plan of a novel according to hints from various quarters," in which the heroine is hurried from one country of Europe to another, always pursued by totally unprincipled young men, and, passing through the most terrible adventures, is "worn down to a skeleton and now and then starved to death!"*

Among her early effusions is an amusing little play entitled "The Mystery, an Unfinished Comedy," which is printed in the second edition of the "Memoir." The Austens, as a family, were fond of acting, and many a play, we are told, was performed by the young people at Steventon. They acted during the winter months in the "common sitting-room" where, for lack of space, the audience must have been a very small one. But in summer time the theatre was transferred to a large barn on the further side of Steventon Lane. An old inhabitant, who remembers it, has shown us the flattened mound where it stood.

A leading member of the little acting company was a young Madame de Feuillade, who was a first cousin of Jane's, being a daughter of the Rev. George Austen's only sister, Mrs. Hancock. Her husband, a French Count, perished by the guillotine during the Reign of Terror. She escaped to England and was received into her uncle's house, where she continued to reside for some years, her parents being in India. Eventually she married Henry Austen.

Madame de Feuillade was a clever woman, and

* See second edition of the "Memoir."

highly accomplished after the French rather than the English mode. She took the chief parts in the plays, and her influence must have been an inspiring one. The prologues and epilogues were written by James Austen, and we are told that they were very amusing. How much we should have liked to take a peep into the great barn on a summer evening, more than a hundred years ago, and seen the group of bright young actors!

There is a charming portrait—a miniature—of Madame de Feuillade taken before her marriage when she was about sixteen years of age. We have seen this portrait. The features are small and delicate and the dark eyes have a piquant expression. She wears a low white dress, edged with blue ribbon and a band of the same ribbon is in her hair, which is powdered and dressed high.

Jane Austen enjoyed some unusual privileges in the quiet country parsonage at Steventon. We are told that her " father was so good a scholar that he could himself prepare his sons for the University." " Her mother was a well educated woman and a thorough lady, though she sat darning the family stockings in a parlour into which the front door opened. She loved all country things, and had a vigorous nature and a contented mind that kept her young and cheerful in spirit until extreme old age. She was

MADAME DE FEUILLADE   REV. JAMES AUSTEN

an excellent letter writer." *   In her " was to be found the germ of that ability which was concentrated in Jane but of which almost all her children had a share."

" The home conversation was rich in shrewd remarks, bright with playfulness and humour and occasional flashes of wit." " It was never troubled by disagreements, even in little matters, for it was not the habit of the Austen family to dispute or argue with each other." " Bad grammar Jane never heard," nor " slang, for there was no slang in those days."

Thus circumstanced it is no wonder that even her earliest compositions, however trivial their subject may be, "are characterised by their pure and simple English," and that we see the influence of her happy home in the " unconscious charm of the domestic atmosphere of her stories and the delicate sub-satirical humour which pervades them."

To hear no slang nor bad grammar was indeed an advantage such as no young writer of the present day can command.

Jane, from early childhood, delighted in reading. She was well acquainted with the old periodicals from the *Spectator* downwards, and her knowledge of Richardson's works was the intimate knowledge of an ardent admirer.   " Every cir-

* Family MSS.

cumstance narrated in 'Sir Charles Grandison', all that was ever said or done in the cedar parlour was familiar to her; and the wedding days of Lady L. and Lady G. were as well remembered as if they had been living friends." *
In the "Life" of Lord Macaulay we read that he and his sister adopted Miss Austen's own characters, in a similar way, as living friends and acquaintances. When speaking to each other they frequently employed sentences from her dialogues "to express the idea, or even the business of the moment; using the very language of Mrs. Elton, and Mrs. Bennet, Mr. Woodhouse, Mr. Collins and John Thorpe, and the other inimitable actors on Jane Austen's unpretending stage." When Macaulay's sister married, her husband "used, at first, to wonder who the extraordinary people could be with whom his wife and his brother-in-law appeared to have lived!"

On the upper floor of the parsonage there was a small parlour called the "dressing-room," already alluded to, where Jane used to write her tales. This room belonged exclusively to the two sisters. Here they followed their favourite pursuits—Cassandra had her drawing materials, and Jane her desk and her piano. A piano, we must remember, was a rare addition in those days to the furniture of a modest country parsonage;

* "Memoir," by J. E. Austen-Leigh.

Scenes of Early Writings

but there was a genuine love of music in the Steventon household and the piano had been procured. Jane Austen has often ridiculed the *affected* love of music, but never its real appreciation. We remember how, when Marianne Dashwood had been asked to sing at Barton Park, " Sir John was loud in his admiration at the end of every song, and as loud in his conversation with the others while every song lasted. Lady Middleton frequently called him to order, wondered how any one's attention could be diverted from music for a moment, and then asked Marianne to sing a particular song which Marianne had just finished."

We have held in our hands some music books, carefully preserved in the family, that belonged to Miss Austen. One of them, which is half-bound with mottled paper sides, contains "twelve canzonettes for two voices, by William Jackson, of Exeter," followed by a collection of "Scots songs." On the fly-leaf is written " Jane Austen " in her own small delicate writing. There is a manuscript book in which the music is beautifully and very clearly written, believed to be the work of her hand. It is bound in parchment and bears her name within the cover. It contains, among other pieces, the song entitled " Ask if the damask rose be sweet, " from " *Susannah*, an oratorio by Mr. Handell," and also a minuet by the same composer. Jane, we know, had a sweet singing voice. Did she sing the duets by Jackson, we wonder, with her sister Cassandra?

We call to mind the description of the sisters' "dressing-room" by their eldest niece Anna (afterwards Mrs. Benjamin Lefroy), who visited the parsonage so often as a young child and who wrote: "about the carpet with its chocolate ground, and the painted press with shelves above for books," and mentioned Jane's "piano, and an oval glass that hung between the windows." "Though this child's age," writes her daughter, "was not more than four or five, she could remember hearing 'Pride and Prejudice' read aloud by its youthful writer to her sister. She was a very intelligent, quick-witted child, and she caught up the names of the characters and talked about them so much downstairs that her aunts feared she would provoke inquiry, for the story was still a secret from the elders."* The title then intended for the novel was "First Impressions." It was begun in October 1796, when Jane Austen was not yet twenty-one years of age.

In that same year Jane paid a visit to her brother Edward and his wife, who were then living at Rowling, a small place in East Kent, about a mile distant from Goodnestone, the seat of the Bridges family, to which Mrs. Edward

* Family MSS.

EDWARD AUSTEN (AFTERWARDS KNIGHT)
From the portrait at Chawton House

Scenes of Early Writings

Austen belonged. Jane travelled with her two brothers, Edward and Francis. The journey from Steventon to Rowling was a serious affair in those days, and we find the party stopping twice on the road—first at Staines and then in London, at some hotel in Cork Street. In driving across Kent they would go by way of Sevenoaks, Maidstone and Canterbury, and, before reaching Sevenoaks, would necessarily pass through the village of Westerham.

Who does not remember that Mr. Collins's pompous letter in which he proposes "to heal the breach" between his family and that of Mr. Bennet, was dated from " Hunsford, near Westerham, Kent"? As Jane was hurried along in her post-chaise did her eyes, we wonder, happen to fall upon some neat dwelling with "a garden sloping to the road" divided by "a short gravel walk" and bounded by " green pales and a laurel hedge" which she fixed upon afterwards for Mr. Collins's "humble abode"? And did Goodnestone, or some other fine property, suggest the future " Rosings," the residence of the dignified Lady Catherine de Bourgh?

"Pride and Prejudice" was finished in August 1797; so that it was written in only ten months! There is a letter given in the "Memoir" from Jane Austen's father to Mr. Cadell, the publisher, dated November 1797, in which he describes the work as a "manuscript novel comprising three volumes, about the length of Miss Burney's 'Evelina'" and asks Mr. Cadell if he would like to see the work with a view to entering into some arrangement for its publication, "either at the author's risk or otherwise." This proposal was declined by return of post and so Elizabeth and Darcy, Mr. Bennet, Mr. Collins and Lady Catherine all remained hidden from view, nor was it till fifteen years later that they stepped on to the public stage!

"Sense and Sensibility" was begun in its present form in November 1797 and finished within a year, but "something similar in story and character had been written earlier, under the title of "Elinor and Marianne" and much of this earlier tale is believed to have been incorporated in the new story, so that "Sense and Sensibility" really contains the earliest writing of Jane Austen's that was given to the public. "Northanger Abbey" was composed in 1798. But the manuscripts of both these novels remained like "Pride and Prejudice" hidden out of sight for many years and the genius possessed by their author was known only to her own family and intimate friends. Hence it is that Jane continued to live her quiet, uneventful life, uncourted by the public. Her powers in the meanwhile developed each year, and when, at last, the time arrived for publication she was able to revise and improve the novels so as to satisfy her maturer judgment.

In Jane Austen, the author and the critic were curiously united, and it has been said of her by a shrewd reviewer that she "always brings the bull's eye of her bright common sense" to bear on all the actions of her various characters. These words recall the remark of a well-known contemporary respecting the author of "Waverley." "In my opinion," he said, "Walter Scott's *sense* is a still more wonderful thing than his genius."

Writing of a contemporary work in 1798, Miss Austen says "We have got 'Fitz-Albini.' My father is disappointed—I am not, for I expected nothing better. Never did any book carry more internal evidence of its author. Every sentiment is completely Egerton's. There is very little story, and what there is, is told in a strange unconnected way. There are many characters introduced, apparently merely to be delineated." *

In the following letter she makes fun of dry historical works. She is writing to her friend Miss Lloyd, a sister of the second Mrs. James Austen, whom she is about to visit. "You distress me cruelly by your request about books. I cannot think of any to bring with me, nor have I any idea of our wanting them. I come to you to be talked to, not to read or hear reading; I can do

* "Letters," Lord Brabourne.

Jane Austen

that at home ; and indeed I am now laying in a stock of intelligence to pour out on you as my share of the conversation. I am reading Henry's ' History of England' which I will repeat to you in any manner you may prefer, either in a loose, desultory, unconnected stream, or, dividing my recital as the historian divides it himself, into seven parts : The Civil and Military ; Religion ; Constitution ; Learning and Learned Men ; Arts and Sciences ; Commerce, Coins and Shipping ; and Manners. So that for every evening in the week there will be a different subject. The Friday's lot—Commerce, Coins and Shipping — you will find the least entertaining, but the next evening's portion will make amends. With such a provision on my part, if you will do yours by repeating the French grammar, and Mrs. Stent will now and then ejaculate some wonder about the cocks and hens, what can we want ? " *

Mrs. Stent, we presume, was somewhat like Mrs. Allen, whose " vacancy of mind and incapacity for thinking were such that, as she never talked a great deal, so she could never be entirely silent ; and therefore, while she sat at work, if she lost her needle or broke her thread, or saw a speck of dirt on her gown, she must observe it, whether there were any one at leisure to answer her or not."

* " Memoir.'·

CHAPTER IX

LEAVING STEVENTON

" Still to ourselves in every place consign'd,
Our own felicity we make or find."

TOWARDS the end of the year 1800 the Rev. George Austen decided to hand over the care of the Steventon living to his son James, and to retire with his family to Bath. This resolution seems to have been taken partly on account of his own health and partly on account of that of his wife. It caused much sorrow to his daughters, who were warmly attached to their home. " Coming in one day from a walk, as they entered the room their mother greeted them with the intelligence, ' Well, girls, it is all settled. We have decided to leave Steventon and to go to Bath.' To Jane, who had been from home and who had not heard much before about the matter, it was such a shock that she fainted away. . . . She loved the country, and her delight in natural scenery was such that she would sometimes say it must form one of the delights of heaven."*

But Jane's ready conformableness to the wishes of others, together with her true philosophy, which made her dwell upon the good rather than the evil of life, enabled her to face the new scheme bravely, and we soon find her busy with all the multifarious preparations for the great move.

Before following the family to Bath, we must allude to a bereavement which befell them in the sudden death of a gentleman to whom Cassandra was engaged to be married. A member of the Austen family has left, in manuscript, the following account of the circumstances.

"Among the pupils at Steventon was a certain Thomas Craven Fowle. . . . Between him and Cassandra Austen an attachment grew up which ended in an engagement. He must have been several years her senior, as he was a pupil at Steventon as early as 1779, when she was only six years old. . . . Thomas Fowle took Holy Orders, and as his friend and cousin Lord Craven was the patron of several livings early preferment was hoped for. Thomas Fowle went out to the West Indies with Lord Craven as chaplain to his regiment, and there died from the effects of the climate. I suppose his cousin had obtained the chaplaincy for him, for he said afterwards, in

* Family MSS.

speaking of his death, that if he had known of the engagement he would not have allowed him to run such a risk. I cannot find the date of Thomas Fowle's decease, nor learn how many years the engagement had lasted when it came to so unhappy an end. With it, so far as we know, ended the romance of Aunt Cassandra's life."

Rytorn in Shropshire is mentioned as the living probably intended for Mr. Fowle. There is an allusion in one of Mrs. Austen's letters, written in 1796, to Cassandra's staying in Shropshire, and its seeming likely that she will soon be settled there permanently; and Jane, in writing to her sister on one occasion, remarks that a friend of theirs supposes her to be busy making her wedding clothes. Had not many of Jane's letters been destroyed after her death we should doubtless have found references to this "domestic tragedy." Her tender sympathy with her beloved sister, however, can easily be imagined.

Jane took an active part in all the business relating to the removal from Steventon. Among other matters the faithful John Bond had to be provided with a good place. She writes to her sister, then at Godmersham, of her satisfaction when this had been accomplished. There were also many farewell visits to pay upon friends both rich and poor. The frequent mention in the "Letters" of their

Jane Austen

poorer neighbours shows how much they were cared for by Cassandra and Jane,

Mrs. Austen's only brother, Mr. Leigh-Perrot, and his wife, used to spend a large part of every year at Bath. This brother had assumed the name of Perrot upon inheriting a small estate at Northleigh in Oxfordshire. The Leigh-Perrots' house was in Paragon, and there Mrs. Austen and Jane were invited to stay upon their arrival in Bath, it having been arranged that these two should precede the others, as Mr. Austen had business to detain him in Hampshire, and Cassandra was at that time visiting her brother Edward in Kent.

On the 4th of May, 1801, the move was made. We can fancy Mrs. Austen and Jane in their postchaise, taking a last glance at the parsonage, amidst its cowslip-decked meadows and its tall branching elms and sycamores, and then driving through the village and along the familiar lanes till, by the " Deane Gate," they entered the great western road which was to lead them far from their country life to Bath and the " busy hum of men."

CHAPTER X

BATH

" The elegant city without a parallel in the Kingdom."

Mɪss Aʊstᴇn writes upon their arrival in Bath : "Our journey here was perfectly free from accident or event ; we changed horses at the end of every stage, and paid at almost every turnpike. . . . Between Luggershall and Everley we made our grand meal, and then, with admiring astonishment, perceived in what a magnificent manner our support had been provided for. We could not, with the utmost exertion, consume above the twentieth part of the beef.

" We had a very neat chaise from Devizes ; it looked almost as well as a gentleman's, at least as a very shabby gentleman's ; in spite of this advantage, however, we were above three hours coming from thence to Paragon, and it was half after seven by our clocks before we entered the house.

" Frank, whose black head was in waiting at the

Jane Austen

hall window, received us very kindly, and his master and mistress did not show less cordiality. We drank tea as soon as we arrived, and so ends the account of our journey which my mother bore without fatigue. . . . I had not been two minutes in the dining-room before my uncle questioned me with all his accustomary eager interest about Frank and Charles, their views and intentions. I did my best to give information." *

Let us follow in the wake of this " very neat chaise " gentle reader, alighting, as Jane did, in Paragon.

Those who know Bath may remember that this name is given to the eastern side of a curved street on the slope of a steep hill, whose opposite side, called Vineyards, is raised above the level of the road on a high terrace walk. In Miss Austen's day Paragon consisted of twenty-one houses only, as those at the northern end of the row were then called Axford Buildings. The Leigh Perrots' house, it seems, was No. 1 Paragon, which is nearly opposite a steep passage leading up to Belmont.† At the further end of the street can be seen the green slopes that rise abruptly to Camden Place ; which " Place " is described by a contemporary writer, the grandiloquent Mr. Egan, as a "superb crescent composed of majestic

* " Letters," Lord Brabourne.
† See "Famous Houses of Bath etc.," by J. F. Meehan.

96

Bath

buildings." No wonder that the author of "Persuasion" made Sir Walter Elliot choose this locality for his residence in Bath as being "a lofty and dignified situation, such as became a man of consequence." There, "in the best house in Camden Place," we can fancy the vain-glorious baronet and his daughter Elizabeth rejoicing in their superiority to their neighbours in the size of their drawing-rooms, the taste of their furniture, and the elegance of their card-parties.

In her first letter from Bath, Miss Austen speaks of walking with her uncle to the Pump Room where he had to take "his second glass of water." On leaving Paragon they would pass down Broad Street and High Street, and then entering the paved court that surrounds the Abbey, they would pass by its grand western front, flanked by the two Jacob's ladders, with their ascending and descending angels. "But here," to quote the words of Mr. Egan again, "the scene from 'grave to gay' is changed with almost the celerity of *Harlequin's bat*, and epitaphs and monumental inscriptions are banished for the lively gaiety of the Great Pump Room."

There it stands! a dignified stone edifice; its four tall fluted pillars crowned with Corinthian capitals, supporting a sculptured pediment. We can imagine the busy scene in the courtyard, where sedan-chairs would be carried to and fro

Jane Austen

amid a throng of gaily dressed people continually passing in and out of the two main entrances.

When Miss Austen and her uncle had passed in also, they would find themselves in a long, lofty room lighted by tall windows, and having at each end a large semi-circular arched recess, one containing the musicians' gallery, the other a statue of Beau Nash standing in a niche above a tall clock. Beau Nash! who for fifty years " was literally the King of Bath," and of whom Goldsmith wrote : " I have known him on a ball night strip even the Duchess of Queensberry of her costly lace apron, and throw it on one of the back benches ; observing that none but abigails appeared in white aprons ; and when the Princess Amelia applied to him at 11 o'clock for one more dance refuse, his laws being as he said like those of Lycurgus—unalterable."

In the centre of the long wall, to Beau Nash's left, a stone balustrade fronts an alcove in which the waters, rising in a marble basin, throw up a column of steam, and where the attendants in mob caps and aprons, are busy filling and handing out glasses to the company. We fancy we see " the ever shifting throng of gaily dressed people " pacing up and down the centre of the room, or sitting at small tables with glasses in their hands sipping their water, the ladies attired in soft white muslin dresses trimmed with blue, green or pink

THE PUMP ROOM

ribbons, and wearing small sandalled shoes of the same colour, their heads surmounted by hats of all shapes and sizes, adorned with tall nodding plumes or with great bunches of fruit or flowers. Among these head-dresses the " Minerva helmet " might be seen " trimmed with a wreath of flowers and a bow of blue riband," which had then just come into fashion.* The men, too, have their share of gay attire. The elderly *beaux* still wear the showy embroidered waistcoats, knee breeches, lace ruffles and sparkling shoe buckles of the late eighteenth century, while the younger men, conforming to the newer style, have adopted close-fitting nankeen pantaloons tied above the ankle by a piece of ribbon, and wear long-tailed blue coats adorned with brass buttons, while their necks are swathed in voluminous white muslin cravats.

We can imagine how Miss Austen would observe all these people, noting their talk as they passed and repassed her ; and how, perhaps, as she detected the airs and graces and veiled selfishness of some, or admired the genuine simplicity of others, she might smile at the thought of her portraiture of the Thorpes, the Allens, and the Tilneys, and of Catherine Morland lying hidden away in her travelling trunk. She could not glance at the clock, to see if it were time for her uncle and herself to return home, without remembering that

* See Heideloff's " Gallery of Fashion," 1796–1803.

it was on a bench beneath that very clock that she had placed Mrs. Thorpe and Mrs. Allen when they recognised each other as old acquaintances, and when "their joy on the occasion was very great, as well it might be since they had been contented to know nothing of each other for the last fifteen years." There Mrs. Thorpe had expatiated upon the beauty of her daughters and the accomplishments of her sons. While poor Mrs. Allen, who "had no similar triumphs to press on the unwilling and unbelieving ear of her friend," was "forced to sit and appear to listen to all these maternal effusions, consoling herself, however, with the discovery, which her keen eyes soon made, that the lace on Mrs. Thorpe's pelisse was not half so handsome as that on her own."

Perhaps when Miss Austen and her uncle quitted the Pump Room they may have made their way through the Pump Yard to the archway opposite Union Passage, and there have had their progress arrested, as it once befell Isabella Thorpe and Catherine Morland, by the difficulties of crossing Cheap Street at this point, thronged as it is "by carriages, horsemen, and carts." If so, Jane would certainly call to mind her introduction of John Thorpe on to the scene of action, when he appeared driving his gig along the bad pavement "with all the vehemence that could most fitly endanger the lives of himself, his companion, and his horse." How well we all know that "stout young man of middling height, who, with a plain face and ungraceful form, seemed fearful of being too handsome unless he wore the dress of a groom," and can fancy we hear him exclaim: "Look at my horse, Miss Morland. Did you

ARCHWAY OPPOSITE UNION PASSAGE

ever see an animal so made for speed in your life? Such true blood. . . . See how he moves. That horse *cannot* go less than ten miles an hour; tie his legs and he will get on." And Catherine's innocent reply: "He does look very hot to be sure."

Miss Austen speaks of her and her uncle taking their "morning circuit." Perhaps this led them to ascend Milsom Street—a street described in glowing colours by Mr. Egan, whose work on Bath we have already quoted. " Milsom Street," he remarks, " is the very magnet of Bath, the centre of attraction and, till the hour of dinner-time, the peculiar resort of the *beau monde*— where the familiar *nod* and the ' *how do you do* ' are repeated fifty times in the course of the morning. All is bustle and gaiety," he continues, " numerous dashing equipages passing and repass-ing, others gracing the doors of the tradesmen ; sprinkled here and there with the invalids in the comfortable sedans and easy two-wheeled car-riages. The shops are capacious and elegant. Among them the visitors find libraries to improve the mind, musical repositories to enrich their taste and science, confectioners to invite the most fastidious appetite, and tailors, milliners, &c., of the highest eminence in the fashionable world, to adorn the male and decorate and beautify the female, so as to render the form almost of statuary excellence." While another contemporary writer observes : " The population of the principal streets seem to consist of gay folks, shopkeepers, and chairmen. To what can we liken the place on a fine day ? A swarm of bees unsettled—the even-ing flies that dance joyfully in the beams of the setting sun. Almost every individual in the numerous groups you meet seems bursting with

Bath

delight ; the streets resound with their voices. But," he adds gravely, "when I have seen a young lady dashing down Milsom Street, her hat turned up before, her voice loud, her step quick and confident, I own I have felt a little startled. Is there or is there not," he asks, "any other large town where young women indiscriminately run either alone or in groups from one end to the other without any servant or steady friend to accompany them, talking and laughing at the corners of the streets, and walking sometimes with young men only ? "

We see by the above that it was quite in accordance with Bath customs for the young Thorpes and Morlands to go about together unaccompanied by any "steady friend."

As Jane Austen passed up Milsom Street perhaps her eye may have fallen on some hale old admiral standing before a print-shop window which suggested to her mind the incident, afterwards introduced into " Persuasion." of Admiral Croft so standing in amused contemplation of the picture of a boat—"a shapeless old cockle shell " —as he styled it, in which he "would not venture across a horse-pond ! "

Milsom Street is peopled with Jane Austen's characters. The august General Tilney, together with his daughter Eleanor, and her "all-conquering brother" Henry, had apartments there. We fancy them settled in the centre of some imposing-looking buildings on the eastern side of the street which are adorned with fluted pilasters and many a stately carving above door and window.

At the top of Milsom Street are Edgar's Buildings, raised upon a high terrace walk and approached by a steep flight of steps. In one of these houses the Thorpes lodged.

Miss Mitford tells us that when she visited Bath she lived far more in the company of Jane Austen's characters than in that of the actual celebrities of the place and found them "much the more real of the two." "Her exquisite story of 'Persuasion,'" she writes, "absolutely haunted me. Whenever it rained, I thought of Anne Elliot meeting Captain Wentworth, when driven by a shower to take refuge in a shoe-shop. Whenever I got out of breath in climbing up-hill, I thought of that same charming Anne Elliot and of that ascent from the lower town to the upper, during which all her tribulations ceased. And when, at last, by dint of trotting up one street and down another, I incurred the unromantic calamity of a blister on the heel, even that grievance became classical by the recollection of the similar catastrophe which, in consequence of her peregrinations with the admiral, had befallen dear Mrs. Croft."

The lively noise and bustle of the streets of

Bath

Bath were agreeable even to the quiet pleasure-seeker like Lady Russell. She had felt the din, made by a merry group of holiday children at Uppercross, to be intolerable ; a din, however, characterised by Mrs. Musgrove, as a "little quiet cheerfulness which was doing her much good." "But," says our authoress, "everybody has their taste in noises as well as in other matters," and "when Lady Russell was entering Bath, on a wet afternoon, and driving through its streets amidst the dash of other carriages, the heavy rumble of carts and drays, the bawling of newsmen, muffin-men, and milkmen, and the ceaseless clink of pattens, she made no complaint. No, these were noises which belonged to her winter pleasures, her spirits rose under their influence . . . and, like Mrs. Musgrove, she was feeling, though not saying, that nothing could be so good for her as a little quiet cheerfulness."

CHAPTER XI

BATH

"Conspicuous for the politeness of its amusements."

In Miss Austen's day there were balls or concerts given on each alternate evening during the season, at the Upper and at the Lower Rooms. The Upper Rooms, situated on the high ground near Belmont, consist of a grand suite of apartments all opening out of each other, and all upon a level with the paved court outside. They were so placed on account of the sedan-chairs, which were carried right into the hall, there to set down their fair occupants.

Miss Austen writes to her sister on May 15 (1801), "I hope you honoured my toilette and ball with a thought (last evening). I dressed as well as I could, and had all my finery much admired at home. By nine o'clock my uncle, aunt and I entered the rooms. Before tea it was rather a dull affair, but then the before tea did not last long, for there was only one dance, danced by four couples. Think of four couples surrounded by

Bath

about a hundred people dancing in the Upper Rooms at Bath. After tea we *cheered up*; the breaking up of private parties sent some scores more to the ball, and though it was shockingly and inhumanly thin for this place, there were people enough, I suppose, to have made five or six very pretty Basingstoke assemblies." In May the Bath season was just drawing to a close, so Jane's experience was very different to that of her heroine Catherine Morland at her first ball in these same rooms during the height of the season. We remember how she and Mrs. Allen slowly squeezed their way through the throng, and how, during the whole evening, poor Catherine could see "nothing of the dancers, but the high feathers of some of the ladies."

The ballroom is little changed since those days. It is thus described by the pompous Mr. Egan : " The elegance of the ball-room (which is a hundred feet in length) astonishes every spectator. The ceiling is beautifully ornamented with panels having open compartments from which are suspended five superb glass chandeliers. The walls are painted and decorated in the most tasteful style; and the Corinthian columns and entablature resemble statuary marble. At each end of the room are placed, in magnificent gilt frames, the most splendid looking-glasses that could be procured to give effect to the general brilliant appearance."

Jane Austen

We have seen this room on a gala night when lighted up by the "five superb glass chandeliers," and we could almost fancy we beheld the "all-

THE MUSICIANS' GALLERY

admired Rauzzini" in his tie-wig, conducting his famous band in the musicians' gallery. We seemed to hear the strains of their music accompanied by the tread of the dancers' feet. "The Monday dress-ball," says a contemporary writer,

Bath

"is devoted to country dances only. At the *fancy-ball* on Thursday two cotillions are danced, one before and one after tea." This *fancy-ball* was not a *bal costumé*, but simply an occasion on which the stringent rules regulating evening dress were relaxed. "In the height of the season," continues our author, "there are generally twelve sets, and as the ladies, on this occasion, exert their fancy to the utmost in the display of their shapes and their dress, the spectacle is magnificent." The ladies, we read, wore comparatively short skirts for the cotillion with their "over-dresses picturesquely looped up." Does not this remind us of Isabella and Catherine "pinning up each other's train for the dance"? A certain Monsieur de la Cocardière, we find, presided over the cotillions. He was a French prisoner-of-war, and, being an accomplished dancer, was a great favourite in the society of Bath.

As Miss Austen moved about the ball-room she must surely have thought of her own Catherine Morland joyfully joining the set on Henry Tilney's arm, when the irrepressible John Thorpe in vain exclaimed, "Heyday, Miss Morland! What is the meaning of this? I thought you and I were to dance together. . . . This is a cursed shabby trick."

In going to the concert or tea-room Miss Austen would cross the octagon-room—the octagon-room so elegant in form and decoration with its domed roof and encircling sculptured frieze, into which the ball-room, the card-room, the tea-room, and the vestibule all open. Here it was that Jane Austen contrived the memorable meeting between Anne Elliot and her sailor lover after their estrangement, when Anne became convinced that he still loved her.

The concert or tea-room is even more ornate than the octagon-room with its many pillars, its statues, its chimney-pieces, carved in rich scrolls, and its long gallery, whose balustrade is of delicate wrought iron. There, on ball-nights, the company adjourned for tea, and on concert nights, for music.

The old Assembly or Lower Rooms no longer exist, having been destroyed by fire many years ago. The author of a Bath Guide which appeared early in the century, speaks of them as situated "on the Walks leading from the Grove to the Parades," and as containing "a ball-room ninety feet long, as well as two tea-rooms, a card-room," and "an apartment devoted to the games of chess and backgammon"; and tells us that they were "superbly furnished with chandeliers, girandoles, &c." Some graceful settees of Chippendale's Chinese pattern are still to be seen that formerly stood in the Lower Rooms. "The balls," writes our author, "begin at six o'clock and end at eleven. . . . About nine o'clock the gentlemen

Bath

treat their partners with tea, and when that is over the company pursue their diversions till the moment comes for closing the ball." Then the Master of the Ceremonies, "entering the ball-room, orders the music to cease, and the ladies thereupon resting themselves till they grow cool, their partners complete the ceremonies of the evening by handing them to the chairs in which they are to be conveyed to their respective lodgings."

It was at a ball in the Lower Rooms, we remember, that Henry Tilney was first introduced to Catherine Morland, and that when he was "treating his partner to tea," he laughingly accused her of keeping a journal in which he feared he should make but a poor figure. "Shall I tell you," he asks, "what you ought to say? I danced with a very agreeable young man introduced by Mr. King; had a great deal of conversation with him; seems a most extraordinary genius." This Mr. King was, it seems, a real personage. He was Master of the Ceremonies at the Lower Rooms, from the year 1785 to 1805, when he became Master of the Ceremonies for the Upper Rooms. A code of rules compiled by him was used for about thirty years. One of these rules, originally laid down by Beau Nash, forbade gentlemen to wear boots in the rooms of an evening. It is said that when a country squire once attempted to defy

Jane Austen

this rule, in the days of the King of Bath, Beau
Nash asked him why he had not brought his
horse into the ball-room, " since the four-footed
beast was as well shod as his master."

The ball-room was used during the daytime as
a promenade, for which it was well suited from its
size and pleasant situation ; its windows commanding extensive views of the Avon winding
amidst green meadows and flanked by wooded
hills. The accompanying reproduction of an old
print taken from a design for a fan, shows the
ball-room when used for this purpose. It was the
fashion also for the company to invite each other
to partake of breakfast at the Lower Rooms after
taking their early baths or first glass of water.

It was in the year 1820 that these old Assembly
Rooms were burnt to the ground. They had
been founded by the great Beau Nash himself,
and had flourished for more than a hundred years.
The last gala held within their walls was singularly
appropriate for the conclusion of their existence.
This gala, consisting of a concert, ball and supper,
and attended by nearly 700 people, was given to
celebrate the eightieth birthday of Mrs. Piozzi,
who, as Mrs. Thrale, was so prominent a figure in
the London and Bath society of the latter end of
the eighteenth century. When the dancing began,
" the veteran lady led off with her adopted son,
Sir John Salusbury, dancing (according to an eye-

THE LOWER ROOMS

(*From an Old Print in the possession of Mr. J. F. Meehan, of Bath*)

witness) with astonishing elasticity and with all the true air of dignity which might have been expected of one of the best-bred females in society."*

The theatre that Miss Austen knew, and where

THE OLD THEATRE

she placed the meeting between Henry Tilney and Catherine Morland after their misunderstanding when they conversed in Mrs. Allen's box, was not the present Bath theatre but the old theatre in Orchard Street. There Mrs. Siddons had first made a name, and there John Kemble,

* See ' Piozziana," by a friend, 1883.

Jane Austen

Foote and many another well-known actor had performed; there, too, Sheridan's "Rivals" achieved a brilliant success after its cold reception in London. The building is still standing, but it has passed through some strange vicissitudes. In 1809, soon after the erection of the new theatre, it was converted into a Roman Catholic chapel, and so remained for fifty-four years, when it became a Freemasons' Hall. Some traces, however, of its early origin seem still to cling to the place, for, looking at it from the street, we noticed what Dickens has termed a " furtive sort of door with a curious up-all-night air about it," which an old print shows to have been once the pit entrance.

In Miss Austen's day the "White Hart" and the "York House" were the chief inns and coaching houses of Bath. The "White Hart" stood in Stall Street facing the Pump Room. It was pulled down in 1867, and replaced by a big modern hotel. We have, however, seen a print of the old inn that hangs in the Pump Room, in which it is represented as a large flat stone building with a pillared portico in the centre, upon which stands the figure of a white hart. As we looked at the long rows of windows in the print, we wondered which of them belonged to the spacious parlour occupied by the Musgrove family, in which the momentous scene in "Persuasion" took place, when Captain Wentworth, overhearing Anne Elliot's words to Captain Harville, writes the letter to her which reopens a world of happiness to them both.

In one of her letters Miss Austen remarks · "On Sunday we went to church twice, and after evening service walked a little in the Crescent Fields." Probably the "church" here mentioned was the Octagon Chapel, the favourite place of worship, in her day, of the visitors to Bath. It stands in Milsom-street at the end of a passage guarded by some iron gates, and would be on her way from Paragon to the Crescent Fields (now the Victoria Park). The building is no longer used as a chapel, but when we saw it a few years ago it was a quaint old-world place, with high pews, deep galleries, and pulpit, all of dark polished wood. The light came down from a lanthorn in the centre of the roof, and we noticed six curious recesses ranged beneath the galleries. These recesses "were really neatly furnished rooms, with chairs, tables, and all necessary comforts." An old advertisement announces that during the winter season "six fires are constantly kept burning" in them "for the benefit of invalids." The organ stands in the western gallery, and there William Herschel performed as organist for some years. He had, however, given up music for astronomy before Miss Austen's day.

Jane Austen

Mrs. Piozzi, who lived for a time in Bath, writes to a friend : " You will rejoice to hear that I came out alive from the Octagon Chapel, where Rider, Bishop of Gloucester, preached on behalf of the missionaries to a crowd, such as in my long life I never witnessed. We were packed like seeds in a sunflower."*

In going towards the Crescent Fields, Miss Austen would proceed along George Street, and then would turn up steep Gay Street, whence a fine view of Beechen Cliff is to be had, "that noble hill," she writes, " whose beautiful verdure and hanging coppice render it so striking an object from almost every opening in Bath." It was on Beechen Cliff that Catherine Morland was walking with the Tilneys when Henry discoursed upon the picturesque in Nature—talking of " foregrounds, distances, second distances, side-screens and perspective, lights and shades, and Catherine was so hopeful a scholar, that when they gained the top of Beechen Cliff, she voluntarily rejected the whole city of Bath as unworthy to make part of a landscape."

The upper end of Gay Street opens into the Circus, which stands on very high ground. Miss Burney has truly styled Bath "a city of palaces, a town of hills and a hill of towns." From the Circus Miss Austen and her friends would pass

* " Famous Buildings of Bath and District," by J. F. Meehan.

Bath

by Brock Street into the Royal Crescent, and so into the Crescent Fields. "At all times the Crescent," writes Mr. Egan, "is an attractive promenade for the visitors of Bath ; but in the season on a Sunday it is also crowded with fashionables of every kind ; and with the addition of the splendid barouche, dashing curricle, elegant tandem, and gentlemen on horseback, the Royal Crescent strongly reminds the spectator of Hyde Park and Kensington Gardens when adorned with all their brilliancy of company." The "Crescent Fields" slope down towards the Avon, commanding beautiful views of the winding river and surrounding country. Although their name has been changed they are probably little altered since Miss Austen strolled about them on that Sunday afternoon in May a hundred years ago.

CHAPTER XII

BATH

" . . . the finished garden to the view
Its vistas opens."

DURING the summer of 1801 the Austens took possession of their new house, No. 4 Sydney Place. Sydney Place lies at the further end of Pulteney Street, flanking a part of the Sydney Gardens. Jane had always liked this situation but had feared the houses there would prove too expensive for the family means. "It would be very pleasant," she had written before leaving Steventon, "to be near the Sydney Gardens. We could go into the labyrinth every day."

We have visited the house in Sydney Place, and have sat in the pretty drawing-room with its three tall windows overlooking the Gardens. The morning sun was streaming in at these windows and falling upon the quaint empire furniture which adorns the room, and which pleasantly suggests the Austens' sojourn there. The house is roomy and commodious. Beneath the drawing-room, which is on the first floor, are the dining-room and

A CORNER OF THE DRAWING-ROOM AT 4 SYDNEY PLACE

arched hall from which a passage leads to a garden at the back of the house. The large, old-fashioned kitchen, with its shining copper pans and its dresser, laden with fine old china, looked as if it had remained untouched since the Austens' day.

The Sydney Gardens have lost none of their charms since it was said of them long ago that "the hand of taste is visible in every direction." There are sloping lawns, and shady walks under the boughs of fine trees. A classical pavilion with a pillared front crowns the summit of a green bank, and, near at hand, the waters of the Kennet and Avon Canal pass beneath the arch of an old stone bridge. "Upon gala-nights," writes Mr. Egan, "the music, singing, cascades, transparencies, fireworks, and superb illuminations, render these gardens very similar to Vauxhall." Miss Austen mentions one of these galas in a letter, remarking that the "fireworks were really beautiful, surpassing her expectations, and that the illuminations too were very pretty."

In a playful letter to her sister, written from Bath, Jane Austen says, "Benjamin Portal is here. How charming that is! I do not exactly know why, but the phrase followed so naturally that I could not help putting it down.

"I am very glad you liked my lace, and so are you and so is Martha, and we are all glad together. I have got your cloak home, which is quite delightful—as delightful, at least, as half the circumstances which are called so.

". . . . We walked to Weston one evening last week and liked it very much. Liked *what* very much? Weston? No, *walking* to Weston, I have not expressed myself properly."

In another letter of later date she writes: "The friendship between Mrs. Chamberlayne and me which you predicted has already taken place, for we shake hands whenever we meet. Our grand walk to Weston was again fixed for yesterday, and was accomplished in a very striking manner. Every one of the party declined, under some pretence or other, except our two selves, and we had therefore a *tête-à-tête*, but *that* we should equally have had after the first two yards had half the inhabitants of Bath set off with us.

" It would have amused you to see our progress. We went up by Sion Hill, and returned across the fields. In climbing a hill Mrs. Chamberlayne is very capital; I could with difficulty keep pace with her, yet would not flinch for the world. On plain ground I was quite her equal. And so we posted away under a fine hot sun, *she* without any parasol or any shade to her hat, stopping for nothing and crossing the Churchyard at Weston with as much expedition, as if we were afraid of being buried alive." *

* " Letters," Lord Brabourne.

VESTIBULE AT 4 SYDNEY PLACE

Bath

The name of " Weston " naturally brings to our
mind the idea of Mrs. Elton and her " exploring
parties " with " Selina " and Mr. Suckling in the
" barouche-landau," of which she boasted to
Emma ; but their expedition was to King's Weston
in the vicinity of Bristol, and not to the little
village of Weston near to Bath.

" My morning engagement," Jane writes, " was
with the Cookes and our party consisted of
George and Mary, a Mr. L., Miss B., who had
been with us at the concert, and the youngest Miss
W. . . . Mary W.'s turn is actually come to be
grown up, and have a fine complexion, and wear
great square muslin shawls. I have not expressly
enumerated myself among the party, but there I
was ; and my cousin George was very kind, and
talked sense to me every now and then, in the
intervals of his more animated fooling with Miss
B., who is very young and rather handsome. . . .
There was a monstrous deal of stupid quizzing
and commonplace nonsense talked, but scarcely
any wit ; all that bordered on it or on sense came
from my cousin George, whom, altogether, I like
very well. Mr. B. seems nothing more than a tall
young man." *   This " Cousin George " was the
Rev. George Leigh Cooke, afterwards well known
and respected at Oxford. As " Tutor in Corpus
Christi College, he became instructor to some of

* " Letters," Lord Brabourne.

129

Jane Austen

the most distinguished undergraduates of his time :
amongst others to Dr. Arnold, the Rev. John
Keble, and Sir John Coleridge." *

"When I tell you I have been visiting a
countess this morning," Miss Austen continues,
"you will immediately with great justice but no
truth, guess it to be Lady Roden—No ; it is Lady
Leven, the mother of Lord Balgonie. On receiv-
ing a message from Lord and Lady Leven, through
the Mackays, declaring their intention of waiting
on us, we thought it right to go to them. I hope
we have not done too much, but the friends and
admirers of Charles must be attended to. They
seem very reasonable good sort of people, very
civil and full of his praise. We were shown at first
into an empty drawing-room, and presently in came
his lordship. . . . He is a tall gentleman-like
looking man, with spectacles and rather deaf. After
sitting with him ten minutes we walked away ;
but Lady Leven coming out of the dining-parlour
as we passed, we were obliged to attend her back
to it, and pay our visit over again. . . . By this
means we had the pleasure of hearing Charles's
praises twice over. There was a pretty little Lady
Marianne of the party, to be shaken hands with
and asked if she remembered Mr. Austen." †

Charles Austen was, at that time, first lieutenant

* " Memoir," by J. E. Austen-Leigh.
† "Letters," Lord Brabourne.

of the *Endymion*, and in that capacity he had
shown attention and kindness to some of Lord
Leven's family.

Here is an allusion to her brother Henry. " I
wrote to Henry," she says, " because I had a
letter from him in which he desired to hear from
me very soon. His to me is most affectionate
and kind, as well as entertaining ; there is no merit
to him in *that;* he cannot help being amusing.
He offers to meet us on the sea-coast if the plan
of which Edward gave him some hint takes place.
Will not this be making the execution of such a
plan more desirable and delightful than ever?
He talks of the rambles we took together last
summer with pleasing affection."

Whilst residing in Bath, Jane Austen wrote the
unfinished tale of "The Watsons," which is given in
the second edition of the " Memoir." " The Watsons," though only a sketch, contains characters
such as Jane Austen alone could have created,
and we part from Tom Musgrave, Emma Watson,
herself, Mr. Howard, Lord Osborne and little
Charles, after so brief an acquaintance, with great
regret. The inn in the " town of D. in Surrey,"
where the ball takes place, which is so admirably
described, was intended, we understand, for the
" Red Lion " at Dorking. Miss Austen sometimes visited her cousins, the Cookes, at Bookham,
and there she would have been within reach of

Jane Austen

Dorking and also of Box Hill, the scene of the unlucky picnic in " Emma."

In 1803 " Northanger Abbey " was sold to a Bath publisher (Bull, of the Circulating Library, it is believed) for the modest sum of ten pounds. But it did not appear before the public, as might have been expected, but remained for several years hidden away in some dusty drawer in the publisher's office. When, however, Jane Austen's fame, as a writer, was becoming established, she desired to recover the copyright of this early work, " One of her brothers undertook the negotiation. He found the purchaser very willing to receive back his money, and to resign all claim to the copyright. When the bargain was concluded and the money paid, but not till then, the negotiator had the satisfaction of informing him that the work, which had been so lightly esteemed, was by the author of " Pride and Prejudice." *

* " Memoir," by J. E. Austen-Leigh.

CHAPTER XIII

LYME

" This other Eden, demi-paradise,
This fortress built by Nature for herself."

In the Autumn of 1804 Miss Jane Austen,
together with her father and mother, spent some
weeks at Lyme Regis. As they drove to that
place from Bath, they would probably go by way
of Shepton Mallet, Somerton and Crewkerne, and,
leaving Axminster a couple of miles to their right,
would join the Lyme Road where an old inn
called "The Hunter's Lodge" stands. Then
passing through the "cheerful village of Uplyme"
they would descend the long hill towards Lyme
itself, and pass down its quaint main street, which
seems to be "almost hurrying into the water" as
Miss Austen says. Half way down the street the
chaise would turn into a lane, which, running
westward, finally makes a precipitous descent to
the harbour. At the end of the little parade or
"walk" nearest to the harbour on a grassy hillside there stands a long, rambling, white cottage,

Jane Austen

and it is in this cottage that tradition declares the Austens to have stayed.

Strangely enough, two members of the family, visiting Lyme in later years to trace the places of which Miss Austen speaks, lodged in this very house without being aware of its associations. One of these, Miss Lefroy, writes, " Leaving the town on our left we followed a road which took us down the steepest and stoniest pitch we had as yet encountered, at the bottom of which we turned into a little bit of street, so narrow that there was only just room for the carriage to pass, out of which we descended on the Esplanade and drew up at our lodgings. And such lodgings ! Surely no other town but Lyme could have supplied them. They were very clean, and the cooking and attendance were good ; but the house was nothing but a queer, ramshackle cottage with low rooms and small windows, and a staircase so narrow and steep and twisted, and withal dark, that it was a source of danger to get up and down it. Then there were two ground floors, one in its proper place, containing kitchen, entrance and dining room, and the other at the top of the house, containing the bedrooms and back door, which latter opened on to the green hill behind. The drawing - room which, by comparison with the rest, might be called spacious, was on the middle floor, and from thence we had a charming view of

Lyme

the sea and harbour and Cobb on one side, and
of the pretty chain of eastern cliffs, on the other."

We can imagine Miss Jane Austen's delight
in this prospect, of which she afterwards wrote,
"the walk to the Cobb, skirting round the pleasant
little bay, which, in the season, is animated with
bathing machines and company; the Cobb itself,
its old wonders and new improvements, with the
very beautiful line of cliffs, stretching out to the
east of the town, are what the stranger's eye will
seek, and a very strange stranger it must be who
does not see charms in the immediate environs of
Lyme, to make him wish to know it better."

We have entered the doors of the "queer ramshackle cottage," now known as "Mrs. Dean's
house," have climbed its "steep, narrow, twisted
staircase," and stood in its quaint parlour, whose
windows command the view described, seen across
a little terrace garden, gay with flowers.

The evidence that Jane Austen stayed in this
house stands on good authority. It was in 1827,
just ten years after her death, that a certain
Captain Boteler, R.N., came to Lyme to take
the command of the Coastguard Service in that
district. By that time Miss Austen's name as a
writer had become well known and the people of
Lyme were proud of the fact that she had visited
their town. On the captain's arrival this cottage
was pointed out to him, as the house in which she

Jane Austen

had lodged. Captain Boteler died some years ago, but members of his family still reside in Lyme.

HOUSE IN WHICH JANE AUSTEN LODGED

Just below "Mrs. Dean's house" and on the further side of the "walk," there is a white cottage perched on the corner of a sea-wall that juts into

Lyme

the water and seems to lift it and its tiny garden out of the waves. Seagulls hover about the very windows of "Bay Cottage." Behind it stretches the harbour, while, near at hand, are the remains of an old pier. "In a small house near the foot of a pier of unknown date," writes the author of "Persuasion," "were the Harvilles settled." This passage clearly points to Bay Cottage. It lies nearer than any other house to the foot of the old pier in question, and it is, besides, the only house in sheltered Lyme which is so much exposed to weather as to make Captain Harville's "contrivances against the winter storms" necessary. From its windows, alone, moreover, could Captain Benwick have been seen, after Louisa Musgrove's fall on the Cobb, "flying past the house" and towards the town for a surgeon. From "Mrs. Dean's house" Miss Austen would look directly down upon Bay Cottage, and, we can well believe, would be struck by its quaint sea-girt situation and would be likely to choose it for the abode of the good captain and his family.

It was in Bay Cottage that we ourselves lodged during our sojourn in Lyme. Its resemblance to the description of Captain Harville's house had struck us at once, but we soon found that our landlady looked upon the whole matter as settled beyond a doubt. She talked of the Harvilles, the Musgroves, Anne Elliot and Captain Wentworth as if they had been in her house but the season before, and pointing to a bedroom on the first floor, exclaimed eagerly. "That is the room where the poor young lady was nursed." And,

CAPTAIN HARVILLE'S HOUSE

again, showing us a cheerful room on the top storey over-looking the sea and the fishing-boats, remarked, "That was the children's nursery!"

In our little parlour, with its projecting bay window, we fancied the Uppercross party assembled when they called on the Harvilles for the first time and "found rooms so small as none but those who invite from the heart could think capable of accommodating so many," and thought of Anne noticing "the ingenious contrivances and nice arrangements of Captain Harville to turn the actual space to the best possible account, to supply the deficiencies of lodging-house furniture, and defend the windows and doors against the winter storms to be expected." In the evenings we used to fancy the Captain, having finished his more active employments for the time being, sitting down "to his large fishing-net in one corner of the room." What a kindly nature has Miss Austen there described! No wonder that "Anne thought she left great happiness behind her when she quitted the house."

The Cobb lies on the further side of the harbour. It is a massive, semi-circular stone pier upon which are two broad causeways, on different levels, forming the Upper and the Lower Cobb. It has undergone many a repair since Miss Austen walked upon it in 1804, but, nevertheless, a considerable part of the old masonry still exists, which is marked by rough-hewn stones placed vertically. Against some of this old masonry, and about half way along the Cobb, are to be seen the identical "steep flight of steps" where the memorable scene of the accident in "Persuasion" is laid. It

Jane Austen

is said that when Tennyson visited Lyme his friends were anxious to point out to him the reputed landing-place of the Duke of Monmouth, "Tennyson waxed indignant, 'Don't talk to me,' he said, 'of the Duke of Monmouth. Show me the exact spot where Louisa Musgrove fell!'" *

The steps in question are formed of rough blocks of stone which project, like the teeth of a rake, from the wall behind. We can ourselves bear witness to the "hardness of the pavement" below, which Captain Wentworth feared would cause "too great a jar" when he urged the young lady to desist from the fatal leap.

Looking westward from the Cobb the rocky coast leading to Pinny can be seen—Pinny, of which Jane Austen has written in such admiration of its "green chasms between romantic rocks, where the scattered forest-trees and orchards of luxuriant growth, declare that many a generation must have passed away since the first partial falling of the cliff prepared the ground for such a state, where a scene so wonderful and so lovely is exhibited, as may more than equal any of the resembling scenes in the far-famed Isle of Wight."

Could Miss Austen see Pinny, as it now is, she would think it even more "wonderful and lovely" than it was in her day. For since then another great landslip has occurred. "It took place," we

* Article in *Monthly Packet* (1893), by John Vaughan.

Lyme

are told, "on Christmas Day 1839, when over forty acres of cultivated land slowly and silently slipped away to a far lower level. Two cottages were bodily removed and deposited with shattered walls to a considerable distance below the cliffs, while an orchard, which still continues to bear fruit, was transplanted as it stood."*

Looking eastward from the Cobb, the eye dwells upon the "very beautiful line of cliffs stretching to the east of the town." In a valley between the hills lies Charmouth. Miss Austen speaks of "its high grounds and extensive sweeps of country and its sweet retired bay backed by dark cliffs, where fragments of low rock among the sands make it the happiest spot for watching the flow of the tide, for sitting in unwearied contemplation."

In going to Charmouth, Miss Austen would take a pathway on the top of the Church Cliffs, which was the fashionable promenade in her day, but which has long since been washed away by the sea. Even the old church itself is now almost undermined by the waves.

The Parade or "Walk," as it used to be called, runs along the foot of a green hill which "skirts the pleasant little bay" of Lyme from the town to the harbour. At the town end of this "Walk" some thatched cottages nestle under the sheltering hill, and just beyond them stand the Assembly

* Article in *Monthly Packet* (1893), by John Vaughan.

Jane Austen

Rooms perched upon the eastern promontory of the bay. The scene in its principal features is the same as in Miss Austen's day; a sea wall being the only marked addition. A stretch of firm sands, lying between the points of the bay, forms a primitive highway for the heavily-laden waggons bearing freight from the harbour to the town. The sight of the horses up to their flanks in a flowing tide is what Miss Austen must often have looked upon.

The Assembly Rooms used formerly to be thrown open to company during the season twice a week, namely on Tuesdays and Thursdays. "The ball last night was pleasant," Jane writes on September 14, "but not full for Thursday. My father stayed contentedly till half-past nine (we went a little after eight), and then walked home with James and a lanthorn; though I believe the lanthorn was not lit as the moon was up; but sometimes the lanthorn may be a great convenience to him."

In former times there were no lamps on the "Walk," so that as Mr. Austen would have to traverse the whole length of it in returning home "a lanthorn or dark nights" would certainly "be a great convenience."

The ball-room is little changed since Miss Austen danced in it that September evening nearly a hundred years ago. It has lost its three

glass chandeliers which used to hang from the
arched ceiling, but these may still be seen in
a private house in the neighbourhood. The

THE ASSEMBLY BALL-ROOM

orchestra consisted, we are told, of three violins
and a violoncello. We visited the room by day-
light, and felt almost as if it were afloat, for
nothing but blue sea and sky was to be seen from
its many windows. From the wide recessed

window at the end, however, we got a glimpse of the sands and of the harbour and Cobb beyond.

Just outside this recessed window there is a steep flight of stone steps which leads from the Parade down to the beach. In former times this flight was much longer than it is now, part of it having been removed to make room for a cart track. On these steps the author of " Persuasion " effected the first meeting of Anne Elliot and her cousin, when his gaze of admiration attracted the attention of Captain Wentworth. Anne and her friends were all returning to their inn for breakfast, as the reader will remember, after taking a stroll on the beach.

Now the inn to which they were bound we fully believe to have been the " Royal Lion," which stands on the right-hand side about half way up the main street. The circumstances of the story all suggest it rather than the old " Three Cups," the only other inn of importance in Miss Austen's day. From the quaint projecting windows of the " Royal Lion " the ladies would be able to see Mr. Elliot's "curricle coming round from the stable yard to the front door," and could " all kindly watch " its owner as he drove up the steep hill. This would have been impossible from the windows of the " Three Cups," which stood at the bottom of the main street and turned slightly away from it. The " Three Cups " was

Lyme

burnt down in 1844, but we have seen its site and have looked at an old print showing the building and its surroundings.

.The personages introduced to us by Miss Austen are not only her creations they are her friends, and have long since become the friends of her readers, and so we pass and repass from them to their author as if *all* had equally together walked this earth. We look up at the windows of the "Royal Lion" and feel that it would be hardly surprising if we caught a glimpse of Anne's sweet face, or of Mary looking out for the "Elliot countenance," and we also look up the rambling old-world street and almost expect to see Miss Austen herself coming down it. The very sounds of Lyme suggest her day. The town-crier goes his rounds with his bell, and his orthodox shout of "O yes, O yes," announcing all matters of moment, such as the return of the trawlers to the harbour, or the arrival of a collier with coal; while at eight o'clock, each evening, the curfew bell is to be heard tolling in the old church tower on the crumbling cliff.

Miss Austen has spoken in praise of "the wooded varieties" of the "cheerful village of Uplyme." We may fancy her going there by a footpath along the valley through which the little river Lym winds. The ground shelves abruptly down to this stream from behind the houses in the main street; some of whose terrace gardens descend to its banks. In one of the most beautiful of these gardens Mary Russell Mitford, when a child, used to play. She speaks in her "Recollections" of the beauty of this romantic garden and of the mansion rented by her father in 1795, where the great Earl of Chatham once lived. Its large gates surmounted by spread eagles are still to be seen in the main street. Opposite to them stands the tiny cottage of Mary Anning, the girl geologist, who discovered the giant bones of monsters that now stretch their length in our National Museum.

In walking up the valley by the side of the Lym, Miss Austen would pass a part of the stream called "Jordan" with its adjacent green sward known as "Paradise," where the early Baptist settlers baptized their followers. A little higher up she would pass Colway Farm, the headquarters of Prince Maurice during the famous siege of Lyme.

Everywhere in Lyme and its neighbourhood there are tokens of the troublous times through which it has passed, from the conquest of the "Invincible Armada" to the home tragedy of Monmouth's rebellion. But to-day in visiting the little sunny town these great and stirring memories pale before the thought of the work and of the writings of three quiet women—Mary Anning,

Lyme

Mary Russell Mitford, and Jane Austen. Like
Tennyson, we say " Don't talk to me of the Duke
of Monmouth. Show me the spot where Louisa
Musgrove fell ! "

CHAPTER XIV

SOUTHAMPTON

" A grey-walled city by the sea."

A few months after the return of the Austens to Bath a sorrowful event occurred in the death of the head of the family—the Rev. George Austen. He died January 21, 1805.

We have already quoted his grand-daughter "Anna's" description of his appearance in elderly life, and remember how lovingly she dwells upon the beauty of his milk-white curly hair and of his bright hazel eyes. Mr. Austen was buried at Walcot Church, which stands on the eastern side of Bath, its graveyard sloping towards the river Avon.

His widow and daughters "were left in what must be called straitened circumstances," remarks a member of the family, "for he had no private fortune and his wife had but a small one." A few years later Mrs. Austen wrote to her sister-in-law : "One hundred and forty pounds a year is the whole of my own income. My good sons have done all the rest." Jane might well be proud of her brothers, for they "shone in their own homes, were kindly affectioned one towards the other, and as sons most attentive and generous."

The Austens had quitted their home in Sydney Place in the late autumn of 1804, and had removed to a house in Green Park Buildings. On the death of Mr. Austen the widow and her daughters went into lodgings for a time at 25 Gay Street. But towards the close of this same year they left Bath altogether and went to live in Southampton, where they shared a house with Captain Francis Austen and his wife, the captain, of course, being frequently absent at sea.

The new home, which was a "commodious old-fashioned house," was situated in a corner of Castle Square. Mr. Austen Leigh, who visited his relatives there when a boy, writes: "My grandmother's house had a pleasant garden bounded, on one side, by the old city wall; the top of this wall was sufficiently wide to afford a pleasant walk with an extensive view, easily accessible to ladies by steps. . . . At that time Castle Square was occupied by a fantastic edifice too large for the space in which it stood, though too small to accord with its castellated style, erected by the second Marquis of Lansdown. . . . The marchioness had a light phæton, drawn by six, and sometimes by eight, little ponies, each pair decreasing in size, and becoming lighter in colour, through all the grades of dark brown, light brown, bay and chesnut, as it was placed farther away from the carriage. The two leading pairs were managed by two boyish postillions, the two pairs nearest to the carriage were driven in hand. It was a delight to me to look from the window and see this fairy equipage put together, for the premises of this castle were so contracted that the whole process went on in the little space that remained of the open square." *

Miss Austen writes to her sister in the early spring "Our garden is putting in order by a man, who bears a remarkably good character, has a very fine complexion, and asks something less than the first. The shrubs which border the gravel walk, he says, are only sweet-brier and roses, and the latter of an indifferent sort. We mean to get a few of a better kind therefore, and at my own particular desire he procures us some syringas. I could not do without a syringa, for the sake of Cowper's line. We talk also of a laburnum." The line referred to occurs in the "Task." The poet is picturing to himself, during a wintry walk, the beauty of the coming spring, and speaks of

"... Laburnum rich
In streaming gold, syringa, ivory pure."

---

* "Memoir," by J. E. Austen-Leigh.

Southampton

"The alterations and improvements within doors," she continues, "advance very properly, and the offices will be made very convenient indeed. Our dressing-table is constructing out of a large kitchen table belonging to the house, for doing which we have the permission of Mr. Husket, Lord Lansdown's painter—domestic painter I should call him, for he lives in the Castle. Domestic chaplains have given way to this more necessary office, and I suppose whenever the walls want no touching up he is employed about my lady's face." *

We have been to Southampton, following Miss Austen's steps, and have wandered about an open space still called " Castle Square," endeavouring to trace the site of the house and garden—the garden which was " considered the best in the town." But houses and gardens and fantastic castle itself have all disappeared to make room for rows of small dwellings. Before we left the place, however, we learnt on good authority that the best houses stood on the northern side of the square. The old city wall, which bounded the Austens' garden, is still standing, and the view to be seen from its parapet of the wide-spreading Solent and its wooded banks can be little changed since Miss Austen looked upon it nearly a hundred years ago.

* " Letters," Lord Brabourne.

Jane Austen

Miss Mitford, who has so often helped us to realise the surroundings of Jane Austen's homes, visited Southampton in 1812. She writes to a friend : "Have you ever been at that lovely spot which combines all that is enchanting in wood and land and water, with all that is 'buxom, blythe and *debonair*' in society—that charming town

OLD CITY WALL

which is not a watering-place only because it is something better? . . . Southampton has in my eyes," she continues, "an attraction independent even of its scenery in the total absence of the vulgar hurry of business or the chilling apathy of fashion. It is, indeed, all life, all gaiety, but it has an airiness, an animation which might become the capital of Fairyland."

Miss Austen mentions a ball at the Assembly

Rooms in one of her letters. These rooms, we are told by a contemporary writer, were situated near the West Quay, and were very elegantly fitted up. The Long Room, he says, was built in 1761, the Ball Room soon afterwards."

"Our ball was rather more amusing than I expected," Jane writes. . . . "The room was tolerably full, and there were, perhaps, thirty couple of dancers. . . . It was the same room in which we danced fifteen years ago. I thought it all over, and in spite of the shame of being so much older felt, with thankfulness, that I was quite as happy now as then. . . . you will not expect to hear that I was asked to dance, but I was—by the gentleman whom we met *that Sunday* with Captain D'Auvergne. We have always kept up a bowing acquaintance since, and being pleased with his black eyes, I spoke to him at the ball, which brought on me this civility ; but I do not know his name, and he seems so little at home in the English language, that I believe his black eyes may be the best of him."*

In the month of October 1808, sorrow again visited the Austen family in the sudden death of Mrs. Edward Austen after the birth of a child. Jane mourned her loss deeply. She writes to her sister Cassandra, who was at that time staying at Godmersham. "We have felt—we do feel—for

* "Letters," Lord Brabourne.

you all, as you will not need to be told; for you,
for Fanny, for Henry, for Lady Bridges, and for
dearest Edward, whose loss and whose sufferings
seem to make those of every other person nothing.
God be praised that you can say what you do of
him; that he has a religious mind to bear him up,
and a disposition that will gradually lead him to
comfort.

"My dear, dear Fanny, I am so thankful that
she has you with her! You will be everything to
her; you will give her all the consolation that
human aid can give. May the Almighty sustain
you all, and keep you, my dearest Cassandra,
well.

"You will know," she continues, "that the
poor boys are at Steventon. Perhaps it is best
for them . . . but I own myself disappointed by
the arrangement. I should have loved to have
them with me at such a time." Recurring to their
loss, she remarks of her sister-in-law, "It is
sweet to think of her great worth, of her solid
principles, of her true devotion, her excellence in
every relation of life."

Again she writes: "That you are for ever in
our thoughts, you will not doubt. I see your
mournful party in my mind's eye under every
varying circumstance of the day; and in the
evening especially figure to myself its sad gloom;
the efforts to talk, the frequent summons to

Southampton

melancholy orders and cares, and poor Edward, restless in misery, going from one room to another, and perhaps not seldom upstairs, to see all that remains of his Elizabeth.   Dearest Fanny must look upon herself as his prime source of comfort, his dearest friend ; as the being who is gradually to supply to him to the extent that is possible what he has lost.   This consideration will elevate and cheer her."*

It is pleasant to learn that it was soon decided for the "poor boys" to visit their grandmamma and aunt at Southampton.   Miss Jane Austen writes on October 24th, "Edward and George came to us soon after seven on Saturday, very well, but very cold, having by choice travelled on the outside, and with no great coat but what Mr. Wyse, the coachman, good-naturedly spared them of his as they sat by his side."

Mr. Austen Leigh mentions this same coachman, of whom he had a distinct boyish recollection, in the "Vine Hunt."   Speaking of the farmer class of huntsmen he says, "The most remarkable person of this class, or rather of a class peculiar to himself, was old Wyse, a civil, respectful-mannered, elderly man, exceedingly fond of hunting, who drove Rogers' coach every day, Sundays excepted, from Southampton to the 'Flower Pot,' Popham Lane, in the morning, and back to Southampton

* " Letters," Lord Brabourne.

in the afternoon. . . . The first time I was allowed to go out hunting without my father, I was placed especially under his care; and as he used also to drive me to and from Winchester School several times in the year, I came to look upon him as an old friend."

To return to Miss Austen's letter. She says of the little nephews: "*They behave extremely* well in every respect, showing quite as much feeling as one wishes to see, and on every occasion speaking of their father with the liveliest affection. His letter was read over by each of them yesterday, and with many tears; George sobbed aloud, Edward's tears do not flow so easily; but as far as I can judge they are both very properly impressed by what has happened. George is almost a new acquaintance to me, and I find him, in a different way, as *engaging as Edward.*

"We do not want amusement: bilbocatch, at which George is indefatigable, spillikins, paper ships, riddles, conundrums and cards, with watching the flow and ebb of the river, and now and then a stroll out, keep us well employed: and we mean to avail ourselves of our kind papa's consideration, by not returning to Winchester till quite the evening of Wednesday." She speaks of taking her two nephews to church the day before (Sunday) and goes on to say: "The weather did not allow us afterwards to get farther than the quay,

Southampton

where George was very happy as long as we could stay, flying about from one side to the other, and skipping on board a collier immediately.

"In the evening we had the Psalms and Lessons and a sermon at home, to which they were very attentive ; but you will not expect to hear that they did not return to conundrums the moment it *was over*. . . . While I write now George is most industriously making and naming paper ships, at which he afterwards shoots with horse-chesnuts, brought from Steventon on purpose ; and Edward equally intent over the 'Lake of Killarney,' twisting himself about in one of our great chairs.

" . . . *We had a little water party* yesterday; I and my two nephews went from the Itchen Ferry up to Northam, where we landed, looked into the 74, and walked home. . . . I had not proposed doing more than cross the Itchen, but it proved so pleasant, and so much to the satisfaction of all, that when we reached the middle of the stream we agreed to be rowed up the river ; both the boys rowed a great part of the way, and their questions and remarks, as well as their enjoyment, were very amusing. George's inquiries were endless, and his eagerness in everything reminds me often of his Uncle Henry."*

In an account of Southampton published in

* "Letters," Lord Brabourne.

Jane Austen

1805, the writer speaks of a long causeway, planted with trees, called the " Beach." " Near its eastern extremity," he remarks, " is the Cross House and Itchen Ferry ; the former is a small round structure with four divisions or apartments opposite to the principal points of the compass, and intended for the accommodation of passengers waiting for the Ferry-boat. In one of the quarters are the arms of Southampton with the date 1634, but parts of the building are apparently much older." We can picture to ourselves the little party waiting in this quaint building for the boat.

Jane Austen's love for children, and her sympathy with them, appears markedly in her letters. Spoilt children certainly annoyed her, or rather the folly of those who spoilt them, as is shown in her inimitable portraiture of the little Middletons and their mother. But where shall we find a more true and tender account of a child's feelings than in the description of little Fanny Price, when she first arrives at Mansfield Park ? And, indeed, in nearly all Miss Austen's works there is some touch which reveals her intimate knowledge of the child-mind, a knowledge to be gained only through love. How true to nature, for instance, is that picture of the little Gardiners standing upon the stairs to receive Elizabeth Bennet, " whose eagerness for their cousin's appearance would not allow them to wait in the drawing-room, and whose shyness, as they had not seen her for a twelve-month, prevented their coming lower." And, again, we are told that when the good people of Highbury had almost forgotten the adventure of Miss Smith with the gypsies, it maintained its ground in the minds of Emma's little nephews, and "Henry and John were still asking every day for the story of Harriet and the gypsies, and still tenaciously setting their aunt right if she varied in the slightest particular from the original recital."

Here is an account, in one of the "Letters," of a visit from a child acquaintance. "The morning was so wet that I was afraid we should not be able to see our little visitor, but Frank, who alone could go to church, called for her after service, and she is now talking away at my side and examining the treasures of my writing-desk drawers —very happy I believe. Not at all shy of course. . . . What has become of all the shyness in the world? Moral, as well as natural diseases disappear in the progress of time, and new ones take their place. Shyness and the sweating sickness have given way to confidence and paralytic complaints. . . .

"*Evening.* Our little visitor has just left us, and left us highly pleased with her; she is a nice, natural, open-hearted, affectionate girl, with all the ready civility which one sees in the best children in the present day; so unlike anything that I was, myself, at her age, that I am often all astonishment and shame. Half her time was spent at spillikins, which I consider as a very valuable part of our household furniture, and as not the least important benefaction from the family of Knight to that of Austen."

" You rejoice me," she writes to her sister, " by what you say of Fanny. . . . While she gives happiness to those about her she is pretty sure of her own share. I am gratified by her having pleasure in what I write, but I wish the knowledge of my being exposed to her discerning criticism may not hurt my style, by inducing too great a solicitude. I begin already to weigh my words and sentences more than I did, and am looking about for a sentiment, an illustration or a metaphor in every corner of the room. Could my ideas flow as fast as the rain in the store-closet it would be charming."*

* " Letters," Lord Brabourne.

CHAPTER XV

" On scenes like these the eye delights to dwell."

In the month of August 1806, Miss Jane Austen and her mother paid a visit to their relative, the Rev. Thomas Leigh, of Adlestrop, who had just inherited and taken possession of Stoneleigh Abbey in Warwickshire.

The Abbey stands in one of the most beautiful and luxuriant parts of the county, between Kenilworth and Leamington; the Avon winding through its pleasure grounds and deer park. In the mediæval part of the building there is an ancient gate-house, upon which is still to be seen a stone escutcheon bearing the arms of Henry II., the founder of the Abbey.

In the days of the Stuarts the Leighs were ardent Royalists. It was in Stoneleigh Abbey that King Charles I. found a resting-place in 1642. "The King was on his way to set up his standard at Nottingham and had marched to Coventry; but finding the gates shut against him, and that no summons could prevail with the mayor and magistrates to open them, he went the same night to Sir Thomas Leigh's house at Stoneleigh, and there his majesty met with a warm and loyal welcome and right plenteous and hospitable entertainment from his devoted subject Sir Thomas." Was Sir Walter Scott, we wonder, thinking of this same Sir Thomas Leigh when he described the character of his fine old cavalier, Sir Harry Lee, of Woodstock?

STONELEIGH ABBEY

Some of the circumstances of his story curiously tally with those connected with the Royalist owner of Stoneleigh Abbey, and certainly the romantic attachment of the Leighs, as a family, to the Stuarts would have appealed to the imagination of the author of "Waverley." So strong was this attachment, we read, that from the time of the flight of James II. down to the very close of the eighteenth century the Lords Leigh, of each

Stoneleigh Abbey

succeeding generation, kept aloof from all public affairs, refusing even to attend the meetings of Parliament. They lived in complete retirement, amid the memories of former times, and "surrounded by portraits of the fallen family." Among these there was a "likeness of King Charles I., by Van Dyck, which, during the troubled times, was painted over with flowers, and which was only discovered in 1836."

The visit of Miss Jane Austen and her mother to Stoneleigh Abbey is chronicled in the following amusing letter, written by Mrs. Austen to a daughter-in-law, the greater part of which has fortunately been preserved :

"STONELEIGH ABBEY,
"<i>August</i> 13, 1806.

"MY DEAR MARY,—The very day after I wrote you my last letter, Mr. Hill wrote his intention of being at Adlestrop with Mrs. Hill on Monday, the 4th, and his wish that Mr. Leigh and family should return with him to Stoneleigh the following day, as there was much business for the executors awaiting them at the Abbey, and he was hurried for time. All this accordingly took place, and here we found ourselves on Tuesday (that is yesterday se'nnight) eating fish, venison, and all manner of good things, in a large and noble parlour, hung round with family portraits. The house is larger than I could have supposed. We

Jane Austen

cannot find our way about it—I mean the best part; as to the offices, which were the Abbey, Mr. Leigh almost despairs of ever finding his way about them. I have proposed his setting up direction posts at the angles. I had expected to find everything about the place very fine and all that, but I had no idea of its being so beautiful. I had pictured to myself long avenues, dark rookeries, and dismal yew trees, but here are no such dismal things. The Avon runs near the house, amidst green meadows, bounded by large and beautiful woods, full of delightful walks.

" At nine in the morning we say our prayers in a handsome chapel, of which the pulpit, &c. &c., is now hung with black. Then follows breakfast, consisting of chocolate, coffee, and tea, plum cake, pound cake, hot rolls, cold rolls, bread and butter, and dry toast for me. The house steward, a fine, large, respectable-looking man, orders all these matters. Mr. Leigh and Mr. Hill are busy a great part of the morning. *We* walk a good deal, for the woods are impenetrable to the sun, even in the middle of an August day. I do not fail to spend some part of every day in the kitchen garden, where the quantity of small fruit exceeds anything you can form an idea of. This large family, with the assistance of a great many blackbirds and thrushes, cannot prevent it from rotting on the trees. The gardens contain four acres and a half. The ponds supply excellent fish, the park excellent venison; there is great quantity of rabbits, pigeons, and all sorts of poultry. There is a delightful dairy, where is made butter, good Warwickshire cheese and cream ditto. One man-servant is called the baker, and does nothing but brew and bake. The number of casks in the strong-beer cellar is beyond imagination; those in the small-beer cellar bear no proportion, though, by the bye, the small beer might be called ale without misnomer. This is an odd sort of letter. I write just as things come into my head, a bit now and a bit then.

" Now I wish to give you some idea of the inside of this vast house—first premising that there are forty-five windows in front, which is quite straight, with a flat roof, fifteen in a row. You go up a considerable flight of steps to the door, for some of the offices are underground, and enter a large hall. On the right hand is the dining-room and within that the breakfast-room, where we generally sit; and reason good, 'tis the only room besides the chapel, which looks towards the view. On the left hand of the hall is the best drawing-room and within a smaller one. These rooms are rather gloomy with brown wainscot and dark crimson furniture, so we never use them except to walk through to the old picture gallery. Behind the smaller drawing-room is the state-bedchamber—

Jane Austen

an alarming apartment, with its high, dark crimson velvet bed, just fit for an heroine. The old gallery opens into it. Behind the hall and parlours there is a passage all across the house, three staircases and two small sitting-rooms. There are twenty-six bedchambers in the new part of the house and a great many, some very good ones, in the old. There is also another gallery, fitted up with modern prints on a buff paper, and a large billiard-room. Every part of the house and offices is kept so clean, that were you to cut your finger I do not think you could find a cobweb to wrap it up in. I need not have written this long letter, for I have a presentiment that if these good people live until next year you will see it all with your own eyes.

"Our visit has been a most pleasant one. We all seem in good humour, disposed to be pleased and endeavouring to be agreeable, and I hope we succeed. Poor Lady Saye and Sele, to be sure, is rather tormenting, though sometimes amusing, and affords Jane many a good laugh, but she fatigues me sadly on the whole. To-morrow we depart. We have seen the remains of Kenilworth, which afforded us much entertainment, and I expect still more from the sight of Warwick Castle, which we are going to see to-day. The Hills are gone, and my cousin, George Cook, is come. A Mr. Holt Leigh was here yesterday and gave us all franks. He is member for, and lives at, Wigan in Lancashire, and is a great friend of young Mr. Leigh's,* and I believe a distant cousin. He is a single man on the wrong side of forty, chatty and well-bred and has a large estate. There are so many legacies to pay and so many demands that I do not think Mr. Leigh will find that he has more money than he knows what to do with this year, whatever he may do next. The funeral expenses, proving the will, and putting the servants in both houses in mourning must come to a considerable sum ; there were eighteen men servants."†

The Lady Saye and Sele ‡ alluded to was a cousin of the Austens, her mother having been a Leigh. It is the same Lady Saye and Sele whom Fanny Burney met "at a rout" in 1782, and of whom she gives an amusing account in her " Diaries. ' This lady seems to have been a sort of " Mrs. Leo Hunter." On being introduced to the author of " Evelina," she exclaimed, " I am very happy to see you ; I have longed to see you a great while ; I have read your performance, and I am quite delighted with it ! I think it's the most elegant novel I ever read in my life. . . . I must

* This "young Mr. Leigh" inherited the Stoneleigh estate. His son Chandos was created Lord Leigh in 1839. † Family MSS.
‡ In 1806 this lady must have been the Dowager Lady Saye and Sele.

Jane Austen

introduce you," continued her ladyship, "to my sister (Lady Hawke), she'll be quite delighted to see you. She has written a novel herself, so you are sister authoresses. A most elegant thing it is I assure you. It's called the 'Mausoleum of Julia!' . . . Lord Hawke himself says it's all poetry. . . . My sister intends to print her 'Mausoleum' just for her own friends and acquaintances."

What ecstasies would Lady Saye and Sele have experienced could she have foreseen the future renown of the young cousin with whom she was walking and talking at Stoneleigh Abbey!

CHAPTER XVI

SETTLING AT CHAWTON

"Rural quiet, friendship, books."

In the course of the year 1809 the Austens left Southampton and settled once more in the heart of Hampshire. Mr. Edward Austen, whom we shall henceforth call Mr. Knight, for he assumed that name about this time, "was able to offer his mother the choice of two houses on his property; one near his usual residence at Godmersham Park in Kent; the other near Chawton House, his occasional residence in Hampshire. The latter was chosen." Chawton Cottage, as it is called, "had been occupied by Mr. Knight's steward, but by some additions to the house, and some judicious planting and screening, it was made a pleasant and commodious abode. Mr. Knight was experienced and adroit in such arrangements, and this was a labour of love to him." *

Miss Jane Austen, writing to her sister from Southampton concerning their future plans, says:

* "Memoir," by J. E. Austen-Leigh.

Jane Austen

"Yes, yes, we *will* have a pianoforte, as good a one as can be got for thirty guineas, and I will practise country dances, that we may have some amusement for our nephews and nieces, when we have the pleasure of their company." Then speaking of "William," a child of about five years of age, she says : "His working a footstool for Chawton is a most agreeable surprise to me, and I am sure his grandmamma will value it very much as a proof of his affection and industry ; but we shall never have the heart to put our feet upon it, I believe I must make a muslin cover in satin-stitch to keep it from the dirt. I long to know what his colours are. I guess greens and purples." *

A few months after this letter was written, Mrs. Austen and her two daughters took possession of their new home. They were accompanied by Miss Martha Lloyd, a sister of Mrs. James Austen, who had come to live with them, upon the death of her mother.

The village of Chawton lies in a specially beautiful part of Hampshire, about five miles from Gilbert White's own Selborne, and, like it, famed for its hop fields and its graceful "hangers" ; while within easy reach is the cheerful little town of Alton. Chawton Cottage stands at the further end of the village, being the last house on the

* "Letters," Lord Brabourne.

CHAWTON COTTAGE

right-hand side of the way just where the Winchester road branches off from that to Gosport, and where a space of grass and a small pond lie in the fork of those roads. Beyond the pond are some thatched cottages with their neat gardens, and to the left, skirting the Gosport road, rise the wooded grounds of Chawton House.

The Cottage is built of brick painted over or white-washed, and has a deep tiled roof and sash windows. The front door opens upon the road, having on each side of it a narrow paled enclosure. We have entered the Cottage and have sat in the very room where Miss Jane Austen used to write—the small parlour on the right-hand side which looks to the front and where the family took their meals. "I heard of the Chawton party," writes a friend to Fanny Knight in 1809, "looking very comfortable at breakfast, from a gentleman who was travelling by their door in a post-chaise." Miss Austen had "no separate study to retire to" Mr. Austen Leigh tells us, "and most of the work must have been done in the general sitting-room, subject to all kinds of casual interruptions. She was careful that her occupation should not be suspected by servants, or visitors, or any person beyond her own family party. She wrote upon small sheets of paper which could easily be put away or covered with a piece of blotting-paper. There was between the

Jane Austen

front door and the offices a swing door which
creaked when it was opened, but she objected to
having this little inconvenience remedied, because
it gave her notice when any one was coming. . . .
In that well-occupied female party there must
have been many precious hours of silence during
which the pen was busy at the little mahogany
writing desk, while Fanny Price, or Emma
Woodhouse, or Anne Elliot, was growing into
beauty and interest. I have no doubt," he adds,
" that I and my sisters and cousins, in our visits
to Chawton, frequently disturbed this mystic process without having any idea of the mischief that
we were doing ; certainly we never should have
guessed it by any signs of impatience or irrit-
ability in the writer."

This "little mahogany desk" is now treasured
by the family of her nephew and biographer. We
have held it in our hands, and have looked upon
the firm, delicate handwriting of its owner in the
manuscript of "The Watsons" which lies within
its narrow drawer.

We learn from one of Miss Austen's letters that
this desk, with all it contained, had once a narrow
escape of being lost. It happened in the autumn
of 1798, when Jane and her parents were halting
for a night at the " Bull and George " at Dartford,
on their way home from Godmersham. Jane
writes to her sister " After we had been here a

PARLOUR IN CHAWTON COTTAGE, WITH JANE AUSTEN'S DESK

Settling at Chawton

quarter of an hour it was discovered that my writing and dressing boxes had been, by accident, put into a chaise which was just packing off as we came in, and were driven away towards Gravesend on their way to the West Indies. No part of my property could have been such a prize before, for in my writing-box was all my worldly wealth, seven pounds. . . . Mr. Nottley immediately despatched a man and horse after the chaise, and in half an hour's time I had the pleasure of being as rich as ever ; they were got about two or three miles off."* Did this adventure, we wonder, befall the manuscript of " Pride and Prejudice "? If so, Jane Austen's readers have yet greater reason to rejoice than even she could have, that the post-chaise was overtaken in time and the little desk rescued.

In the larger parlour at Chawton Cottage Jane's piano must have stood. Her nephew tells us that she was in the habit of practising daily, chiefly before breakfast. " She did so, I believe," he says, " partly that she might not disturb the rest of the party who were less fond of music. In the evening she would sing to her own accompaniment, some simple old songs, the words and airs of which, now never heard, still linger in my memory."

A large garden lay behind the house where, we

* " Letters," Lord Brabourne.

are told, "there was a pleasant, irregular mixture of hedgerow, and gravel walk, and orchard, and long grass for mowing, arising from two or three little enclosures having been thrown together." "I remember the garden well," writes Miss Lefroy. "A very high thick hedge divided it from the (Winchester) road, and round it was a pleasant shrubbery walk, with a rough bench or two where no doubt Mrs. Austen and Cassandra and Jane spent many a summer afternoon."* We have sat in what was once this "shrubbery walk," beneath the shade of great over-arching trees, one of which, an oak, is said to have been planted by Jane herself.

Writing to her sister during the month of May she says : "The whole of the shrubbery border will soon be very gay with pinks and sweet-williams, in addition to the columbines already in bloom. The syringas, too, are coming out. . . . You cannot imagine—it is not in human nature to imagine—what a nice walk we have round the orchard. The rows of beech look very well indeed, and so does the young quickset hedge in the garden. I hear to-day that an apricot has been detected on one of the trees." Was it a "Moor Park," we wonder, such as Mrs. Norris and Dr. Grant quarrelled over?

By the time the family went to live at Chawton,

* Family MSS.

Settling at Chawton

Mrs. Austen had handed over the management of the house-keeping to her daughters. She was then nearly seventy years of age, but "she found plenty of occupation for herself," writes Miss Lefroy, "in gardening and needlework. The former was, with her, no idle pastime, no mere cutting of roses and tying up of flowers. She dug up her own potatoes, and I have no doubt she planted them, for the kitchen garden was as much her delight as the flower borders, and I have heard my mother say that when at work, she wore a green round frock like a day-labourer's." *

We have seen a specimen of Mrs. Austen's needlework, done at this period. It is a large chintz patchwork counterpane of most elaborate design. In the centre is a basket of flowers while landscapes and flowers adorn the border. A black silhouette portrait, taken evidently while she was living at Chawton, enables us to realise the appearance of this bright, spirited, old lady. In looking at it we recall Miss Lefroy's remark that "she was amusingly particular about people's noses, having a very aristocratic one herself."

"It was a very quiet life [at the cottage]," writes Miss Lefroy, "according to our ideas, but they were great readers, and besides the house-keeping our aunts occupied themselves in work-

Jane Austen

ing for the poor and in teaching some boy or girl
to read or write." When, however, the Edward
Knights were visiting their Chawton home, and
the "Great House" was full of life and animation, a new source of enjoyment came into Jane's
quiet life. The "Great House" and the cottage
lie within a few hundred yards of each other,
the gates of the park opening upon the Gosport
road. The house, a fine old Elizabethan mansion, with its Tudor porch, and its heavy mullioned
windows, may be seen by the passer-by, standing
on rising ground; while a little below it, in a
gentle hollow, lies the old church of Chawton—a
small grey stone edifice embowered in trees.

We have visited Chawton House, being kindly
welcomed by the present owner—a son of that
"young Edward" of whom his "Aunt Jane"
writes so affectionately from Southampton. A
large wainscoted room (now the drawing-room),
containing a great chimney-piece of carved wood
and stone, was the hall of the mansion in Miss
Austen's time. How many happy meetings of the
children and their loved "Aunt" must its sombre
walls have witnessed! But the room which is
especially associated with Jane Austen is the
"oak-room" on the first floor, which has a
large recess that stands above the porch. Here
the family often sat of an evening. This room
is unchanged since Miss Austen's day. And

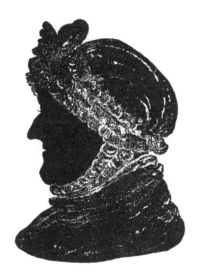

Settling at Chawton

unchanged also must be the great oaken stair-case with its massive balustrade leading to dark mysterious passages, and concealing beneath its steps a secret hiding-place such as would have delighted the heart of Catherine Morland.

The interesting family portraits which now hang in Chawton House hung formerly at Godmersham. That of Edward Austen (afterwards Knight) was taken in Rome, whither he had gone when making the "grand tour" at the age of twenty-one. When looking at this portrait we can well imagine that the original "was not only a very amiable man, kind and indulgent to all connected with him," but that he "possessed also a spirit of fun and liveliness which made him especially delightful to all young people." * The portraits of Mr. and Mrs. Thomas Knight (who adopted Edward), painted by Romney, are fine works of art. Mr. Knight died in 1794, but we find frequent mention in the "Letters" of Mrs. Knight, to whom Jane was much attached.

The windows at the back of the mansion over-look rising lawns dotted about with gay flower borders. At the top of the ascent there is a large old-fashioned kitchen garden, where fruit trees, vegetables, and flowers consort happily together, and where a turf walk, flanked by

* "Memoir," by J. E. Austen-Leigh.

hedges of dahlias, sunflowers, and white Japanese anemones, with a sun-dial in its centre, leads up to a yew arbour. How often must Miss Austen have sat in that arbour enjoying the sights around her!

CHAPTER XVII

CHAWTON

"Nor Fame I slight, nor for her favours call ;
She comes unlook'd for, if she comes at all."

Soon after the family were settled at Chawton, Miss Jane Austen began to revise her earlier novels for the press, and in the spring of 1811 we find her already occupied with correcting the proof sheets of " Sense and Sensibility."   In the month of April she paid a visit to her brother Henry in London, and she writes to her sister Cassandra, who evidently supposed she might be too busy with London engagements to think much of her book in the printer's hands, " No, indeed, I am never too busy to think of S. and S.   I can no more forget it than a mother can forget her sucking child and I am much obliged to you for your inquiries.   I have had two sheets to correct, but the last only brings us to Willoughby's first appearance.   Mrs. K.* regrets, in the most flattering manner, that she must wait *till* May, but I have

* Mrs. Thomas Knight.

183

scarcely a hope of its being out in June. Henry does not neglect it; he has hurried the printer, and says he will see him again to-day. . . . I am very much gratified by Mrs. K.'s interest in it. . . . I think she will like my Elinor, but cannot build on anything else."

"Sense and Sensibility" was published in the course of this same year (1811). From the accompanying facsimile of the title-page of the first edition, it will be seen that the work was "Printed for the Author, by C. Roworth, Bell-yard, Temple-bar, and published by T. Egerton, Whitehall." It is evident, therefore, that the publisher would take no risk in the transaction and that the novel was produced at the author's expense. It is the only one of the novels so published, for on the title-pages of "Pride and Prejudice" and of "Mansfield Park" we find the words "Printed for T. Egerton," and on those of the later novels "Printed for John Murray." The reader will notice that the novel is announced simply as "By a Lady." These words never again appeared on any title-page of Jane Austen's works. In its later editions, "Sense and Sensibility" is announced as "by the Author of 'Pride and Prejudice,'" and when "Pride and Prejudice" itself first appeared it was announced as "By the Author of 'Sense and Sensibility.'"

Mr. Austen Leigh tells us that he had "no

SENSE

AND

SENSIBILITY:

A NOVEL.

IN THREE VOLUMES.

———

BY A LADY.

———

VOL. I.

———

London:

PRINTED FOR THE AUTHOR,

By C. Roworth, Bell-yard, Temple-bar,

AND PUBLISHED BY T. EGERTON, WHITEHALL.

1811.

record of the publication of 'Sense and Sensibility,'" and in a letter dated November 1813, Jane remarks to her sister "Your tidings of S. and S. give me pleasure, I have never seen it advertised." We have been fortunate enough to discover an announcement of its publication in a copy of the *Edinburgh Review* for November 1812. It appears under the heading of "Novels" in the "Quarterly List of New Publications from July to November." The following is a facsimile of the entry.

NOVELS.

Traits of Nature. By Miss Burney. 5 vol. 1*l*. 10s.
I'll Consider of It. A Tale. 3 vol. 21s.
Pleasant Adventures of Gusman of Alfarache, from the Spanish. 3 vol. 15s.
Bouverie, or the Pupil of the World. 5 vol. 1*l*. 7s. 6d.
The Loyalists. By Mrs West. 3 vol. 21s.
Self-Indulgence; a Tale of the 19th Century. 2 vol. 12s.
Friends Unmasked, or Scenes in Real Life; founded on facts. By Miss A. A. Hutchinson. 3 vol. 12mo. 20s.
Cottage Sketches, or Active Retirement. 2 vol. 9s.
Raphael, or Peaceful Life. By Mr Green, 2 vol. 10s.
Edgeworth's Tales of Fashionable Life. Vol. 4, 5, 6. 21s.
Sense and Sensibility. By a Lady. 3 vol. 15s.
Things by their Right Names. By A Person without a Name. 2 vol.
Notoriety, or Fashionables Unveiled. 3 vol. 18s.
The Serious Family, or What do You think of the World. 3 vol. 18s.
I says, says I. By Thinks I to Myself. 2 vol. 10s. 6d.

It is interesting to see that the announcement which immediately precedes that of "Sense and Sensibility" is of vols. iv., v., and vi. of Miss Edgeworth's "Tales of Fashionable Life," which

Jane Austen

include her delightful story of the "Absentee,"
while in the same list we find the "Loyalists" by
Mrs. West. Jane, writing playfully to a niece in
1814, remarks: " I am quite determined not to be
pleased with Mrs. West's 'Alicia de Lacy,' should
I ever meet with it, which I hope I shall not.   I
think I can be stout against anything written by
Mrs. West.   I have made up my mind to like no
novels really but Miss Edgeworth's, yours and
my own."

Another entry in the above list is that of
"Traits of Character," by Miss Burney; not
Fanny Burney, who became Madame D'Arblay
in 1793, but her half-sister, a Miss S. H. Burney.
She had previously written a novel called
"Clarentine." "We are reading 'Clarentine,'"
Jane wrote in 1807, "and are surprised to find
how foolish it is. . . . It is full of unnatural con-
duct and forced difficulties, without striking merit
of any kind."

Under the heading "Poetry," in this same
quarterly "List of New Publications," we find
"Tales. By G. Crabbe. 8vo, 12s." Miss Austen
"thoroughly enjoyed Crabbe," her nephew tells
us, "perhaps on account of a certain resemblance
to herself in minute and highly-finished detail."

In No. XL. of the *Edinburgh Review*, the same
which contains the foregoing announcements, appears Lord Jeffrey's critique upon the " Rejected

Addresses," which had just taken the public by surprise. There is an allusion to that work in one of the "Letters." A Mrs. —— having observed that she had sent a copy of the "Rejected Addresses" to a friend, Jane writes: "I began talking to her a little about them, and expressed my hope of their having amused her. Her answer was 'Oh dear, yes, very much; very droll indeed; the opening of the house and the striking up of the fiddles!' What she meant, poor woman, who shall say?"

"Pride and Prejudice" was published early in 1813. Jane Austen writes to her sister from Chawton, January 29: "I hope you received my little parcel by J. Bond * on Wednesday evening, my dear Cassandra, and that you will be ready to hear from me again on Sunday, for I feel that I must write to you again to-day. I want to tell you that I have got my own darling child from London. On Wednesday I received one copy sent down by Falkener, with three lines from Henry to say that he had given another to Charles and sent a third by the coach to Godmersham. . . . The advertisement is in our paper to-day for the first time: 18s. He shall ask £1 1s. for my two next, and £1 8s. for my stupidest of all. Miss B. dined with us on the very day of the

---

* The old servant and factotum of her father in the Steventon days.

book's coming out, and in the evening we fairly set at it, and read half the first vol. to her, prefacing that, having intelligence from Henry that such a work would soon appear, we had desired him to send it whenever it came out, and I believe it passed with her unsuspected. She was amused, poor soul! *That* she could not help, you know, with two such people to lead the way, but she really does seem to admire Elizabeth. I must confess that I think her as delightful a creature as ever appeared in print, and how I shall be able to tolerate those who do not like *her* at least, I do not know. . . . I am exceedingly pleased that you can say what you do, after having gone through the whole work, and Fanny's praise is very gratifying. My hopes were very strong of *her* but nothing like a certainty. Her liking Darcy and Elizabeth is enough. She might hate all the others if she would. I have her opinion under her own hand this morning, but your transcript of it, which I had first, was not, and is not, the less acceptable. To *me* it is, of course, all praise, but the more exact truth which she sends *you* is good enough." *

Shortly after this letter was written we find Jane, when on a visit to her brother Henry, in London, looking out for portraits in the picture galleries, that may bear some resemblance to her

* " Memoir," by J. E. Austen-Leigh.

CHAWTON HOUSE

ideal characters. "Henry and I," she writes, "went to the Exhibition in Spring Gardens. It is not thought a good collection, but I was very well pleased, particularly (pray tell Fanny) with a small portrait of Mrs. Bingley, excessively like her. I went in hopes of seeing one of her sister, but there was no Mrs. Darcy. Perhaps, however, I may find her in the great exhibition, which we shall go to if we have time. I have no chance of her in the collection of Sir Joshua Reynolds's paintings, which is now showing in Pall Mall, and which we are also to visit.

"Mrs. Bingley is exactly herself—size, shaped face, features and sweetness; there never was a greater likeness. She is dressed in a white gown with green ornaments, which convinces me of what I always supposed, that green was a favourite colour with her. I daresay Mrs. D. will be in yellow." Finishing her letter later in the day she adds: "We have been both to the exhibition and to Sir Joshua Reynolds's, and I am disappointed, for there was nothing like Mrs. D. at either. I can only imagine that Mr. D. prizes any picture of her too much to like it should be exposed to the public eye. I can imagine he would have that sort of feeling—that mixture of love, pride and delicacy." *

Apropos of "Pride and Prejudice" a question

* "Letters," Lord Brabourne.

has arisen as to whether Mr. Collins had a proto-
type in a certain Bishop Porteus, who held the
living of Hunton, in Kent, towards the close of the
eighteenth century. This pompous divine has
left private "Reminiscences," in which we are
told the "diction, manner, and matter" are
simply those of Mr. Collins himself. It is quite
possible that Miss Austen may have heard anec-
dotes of his sayings and doings when visiting her
brother in Kent, and that these suggested to her
mind the portraiture of some such character as
his. But we know beyond a doubt that she
"drew from nature but never from individuals";
therefore the existence of Dr. Porteus only
proves that in the delineation of Mr. Collins,
which has been termed "one of the most distinct
and original portraits in the great gallery of
fiction," she was no caricaturist, but a faithful
student of nature.

When "Pride and Prejudice" appeared before
the public, its author was already far advanced
in the composition of "Mansfield Park." Here is
an allusion to the story in a letter dated February,
1813, written at Chawton. After describing a
rather dull party at which she had been present,
Miss Austen goes on to say, "As soon as a
whist party was formed, and a round table
threatened, I made my mother an excuse, and
came away, leaving just as many for *their* round

table as there were at Mrs. Grant's. I wish they might be as agreeable a set."

Who does not call to mind the players at "Speculation" gathered round Mrs. Grant's table when Henry Crawford, "pre-eminent in all the lively turns, quick resources, and playful impudence that could do honour to the game," was directing the play of both Fanny and Lady Bertram, trying to inspire the one with "avarice and harden her heart (which where William was concerned was a difficult matter), and to prevent the other from ever looking at her cards."

In March 1814 we find Jane reading "Mansfield Park" for the first time to her brother Henry, as they were seated together in a postchaise on their way to London. She writes on the following day to her sister, "We had altogether a very good journey, and everything at Cobham was comfortable. . . . We did not begin reading till Bentley Green. Henry's approbation is hitherto even equal to my wishes. He says it is different from the other two. but does not appear to think it at all inferior. He has only married Mrs. R. I am afraid he has gone through the most entertaining part. He took to Lady B. and Mrs. N. most kindly, and gives great praise to the drawing of the characters. He understands them all, likes Fanny, and I think, foresees how it will all be. . . . He admires H. Crawford: I mean properly, as a clever, pleasant man.   I tell you all the good I can as I know how much you will enjoy it."

As time passed on Miss Austen enjoyed a new pleasure in the more equal companionship of her elder nephews and nieces, who were now growing up.   The removal to Chawton had brought her within easy reach of her brother James and his family, who were still at Steventon, as well as of the Knights when they visited their Chawton home.

Miss Lefroy, a grand-daughter of the Rev. James Austen, writes,* " As may be supposed a great deal of intercourse was kept up between Steventon and Chawton.   Our grandfather was a most attentive son, and one of the pleasures of my mother's youth was sometimes riding with him to see her grandmother and aunts through the pretty cross roads and rough lanes, inaccessible to wheels, which lay between the two places. . . .   In her Aunt Jane, who was the object of her most enthusiastic admiration, she found a sympathy and a companionship which was the delight of her girlhood, and of which she always retained the most grateful remembrance. . . .   But I will copy my mother's own account.

" ' The two years before my marriage and the three afterwards, during which we lived near

* Family MSS.

VIEW FROM CHAWTON COTTAGE

Chawton

Chawton, were the years in which my great inti-
macy with her was formed; when the original seventeen years between us seemed reduced to seven,
or none at all.   It was my amusement during part
of a summer visit to the cottage to procure novels
from the circulating library at Alton, and after
running them over to narrate and turn into
ridicule their stories to Aunt Jane, much to her
amusement, as she sat over some needlework
which was nearly always for the poor.   We both
enjoyed the fun, as did Aunt Cassandra in her
quiet way though, as one piece of nonsense led to
another, she would exclaim at our folly, and beg us
not to make her laugh so much.'

" To some of that ' nonsense ' the following letter
from Aunt Jane refers.* She and my mother
had been laughing over a most tiresome novel,
in eight volumes, by a Mrs. Hunter, containing
story within story, and in which the heroine
was always in floods of tears."

" Miss Jane Austen begs her best thanks may
be conveyed to Mrs. Hunter, of Norwich, for the
thread paper she has been so kind as to send by
Mrs. Austen, and which will be always very
valuable on account of the spirited sketches (made
doubtless by Nicholson or Glover) of those most
interesting spots, Fairfield Hall, the Mill, and,

* It is needless to say that this letter never found its way to the
post.

above all, the tomb of Howard's wife, of which Miss Jane Austen is undoubtedly a good judge, having spent so many summers at Fairfield Abbey, the delighted guest of the worthy Mrs. Wilson. It is impossible for any likeness to be more complete. Miss J. A.'s tears have flowed over each sweet sketch in such a way as would have done Mrs. Hunter's heart good to see, and if she could understand all Miss Austen's interest in the subject she would certainly have the kindness to publish at least four more volumes about the Hint family, and especially would give many further particulars in that part of it which Mrs. Hunter has hitherto handled too briefly—viz., the history of Mary Hint's marriage with Howard.

" Miss Jane Austen cannot close this small epitome of the miniature of an abridgment of her thanks and admiration without expressing her sincere hope that Mrs. Hunter is provided with a more safe conveyance to London than Alton can now boast ; as the 'Car of Falkenstein,' the pride of that town, was overturned within the last ten days."

CHAPTER XVIII

GODMERSHAM

" Where the deer rustle through the twining brake."

GODMERSHAM Park, in Kent, where her brother
Edward and his family lived, was almost a second
home to Miss Jane Austen as well as to her sister
Cassandra. Jane had been warmly attached to
Edward's wife, and the death of her sister-in-law
increased her devotion to her beloved brother and
to his motherless children.

Godmersham Park lies in a wooded, undulating
country about eight miles south-west of Canterbury, and is watered by the pretty river Stoure.
The house, a long, low building of white stone with
two wings, has a wide portico supported by
columns. We have passed through this stately
entrance, by the kind permission of the present
owner, and have sat in the rooms where Jane sat,
looking, as she must have looked, upon the sunny,
green slopes of the park where deer were feeding
beneath shady trees. A great, square hall occupies the centre of the mansion, rich in carved

doorways which are flanked by white pilasters and surmounted by pediments.

Writing from Godmersham to her sister in 1813, Jane describes the arrival of her sailor brother, Charles, accompanied by his wife and their two children, and tells how they were met and welcomed in this hall. " They came last evening at about seven," she says. " We had given them up, but *I* still expected them. . . . They had a very rough passage. . . . However, here they are, safe and well, just like their own nice selves ; Fanny looking as neat and white this morning as possible, and dear Charles all affectionate, placid, quiet, cheerful, good humour. . . . Cassy was too tired and bewildered just at first to seem to know anybody. We met them in the hall—the women and girl part of us—but before we reached the library, she kissed me very affectionately. . . . It was quite an evening of confusion, as you may suppose. At first we were all walking about from one part of the house to the other ; then came a fresh dinner in the breakfast-room which Fanny and I attended ; then we moved into the library, were joined by the dining-room people, were introduced and so forth ; and then we had tea and coffee which was not over till past ten. Billiards again drew all the odd ones away, and Edward, Charles, the two Fannies, and I, sat snugly talking."*

* " Letters," Lord Brabourne.

HALL IN GODMERSHAM HOUSE

Godmersham

We can picture to ourselves this happy group seated in the library, whose walls are of wainscot, painted white with large and richly framed panels, then filled by the family portraits.

The drawing-room lies at the back of the house. It is a long room with windows down to the ground that overlook flower beds and green lawns which terminate in a long ascending glade on the side of a wooded hill. Here Jane sat writing to her sister one November day: "I am all alone— Edward is gone into the woods. At this present time I have five tables, eight-and-twenty chairs, and two fires all to myself."

With the children of the family "Aunt Jane" was always the centre of attraction. "She was the one to whom we always looked for help," writes a niece. "She could make everything amusing to a child. . . . She would tell us the most delightful stories, chiefly of Fairyland, and her fairies had all characters of their own. The tale was invented, I am sure, at the moment and was continued for two or three days if occasion required—being begged for on all possible and impossible occasions."* Sometimes she composed impromptu verses for their entertainment. She is described as "standing in one of the windows at Godmersham when awaiting the arrival of her brother Frank, and his newly-married wife,

* "Memoir," by J. E. Austen-Leigh.

allaying the impatience of the little nephews and nieces, watching with her, by a poetical account of the bride and bridegroom's journey from Canterbury; the places they passed through, the drive through the park, and the arrival, at last, at the house."

Several members of the Austen family besides Jane were endowed with this faculty of invention —a faculty termed by Mrs. Austen "sprack wit." They often wrote amusing charades to enliven their evening gatherings, when "merry verses and happy, careless inventions of the moment would flow without difficulty from their ready pens." Some of these "charades" have been collected and printed for private circulation. We are permitted to give two of them. The first is by Jane Austen's father. Its solution was unknown to his descendants, but two ingenious answers have been suggested by readers of these pages.

> " Without me, divided, fair ladies, I ween,
> At a ball or a concert you'll never be seen;
> You must do me together, or safely I'd swear,
> Whatever your carriage you'll never get there."
> (Flambeau—Alight.)

The second is by Jane herself.

> " When my first is a task to a young girl of spirit
> And my second confines her to finish the piece,
> How hard is her fate! but how great is her merit
> If by taking my whole she effect her release!"
> (Hemlock.)

"A YOUNG GIRL OF SPIRIT"

Godmersham

Sometimes the evenings at Godmersham were passed in listening to the reading of some notable book. It was in June 1808, just four months after " Marmion " had appeared before the public, that Jane wrote : " Ought I to be very much pleased with ' Marmion ' ? As yet I am not. James * reads it aloud in the evening—the short evening beginning at ten, and broken by supper." But a further acquaintance with the poem made her change her opinion, for writing a few months later of sending out a worked rug to her brother Charles in the West Indies, she remarks : " I am going to send ' Marmion ' out with it—very generous in me I think."

Miss Austen often mentions " Sackree," the children's nurse and a general favourite. " I told Sackree," she writes to her sister, " that you desired to be remembered to her which pleased her ; and she sends her duty and wishes you to know that she has been into the great world. She went on to town after taking William to Eltham, and, as well as myself, saw the ladies go to Court on the 4th. She had the advantage, indeed, of me in being in the Palace."†

Sackree " lived on at Godmersham " Lord Brabourne tells us, " saw and played with many of the children of her nurslings, and died in 1851

---

* He was then staying at Godmersham.
† " Letters," Lord Brabourne.

Jane Austen

in her ninetieth year." We have seen her grave
in the pretty churchyard of Godmersham village
church, where she is described as "the faithful
servant and friend, for nearly sixty years, of
Edward Knight, of Godmersham Park, and the
beloved nurse of his children."

One of Miss Austen's little nieces living to old
age has only recently passed away—Miss Marianne Knight. A cousin of a younger generation,
to whom the old lady used to talk of her early
recollections, records the following words of Miss
Knight :

"I remember that when Aunt Jane came to us
at Godmersham she used to bring the MS. of
whatever novel she was writing with her, and
would shut herself up with my elder sisters in one
of the bedrooms to read them aloud. I and the
younger ones used to hear peals of laughter
through the door, and thought it very hard that we
should be shut out from what was so delightful.
I also remember how Aunt Jane would sit quietly
working beside the fire in the library, saying
nothing for a good while, and then would suddenly
burst out laughing, jump up and run across the
room to a table where pens and paper were lying,
write something down, and then come back to the
fire and go on quietly working as before."

When Miss Austen visited Godmersham in
1813, both " Sense and Sensibility " and "Pride

MR. THOMAS KNIGHT

Godmersham

and Prejudice" had appeared before the public
and much curiosity was felt concerning their
author. "Oh! I have more sweet flattery from
Miss Sharp," Jane writes playfully. "She is an
excellent kind friend, I am read and admired in
Ireland, too. There is a Mrs. Fletcher, the wife
of a judge, an old lady, and very good and very
clever, who is all curiosity to know about me—
what I am like, and so forth. I am not known to
her by name, however. . . . I do not despair of
having my picture in the Exhibition at last—
all white and red, with my head on one side; or
perhaps I may marry young Mr. D'Arblay. I
suppose in the meantime I shall owe dear Henry
a great deal of money for printing, &c."*

We find mention of much pleasant visiting
among friends and neighbours in the "Letters"
written from Godmersham. Sometimes Jane
spends a few days at Goodnestone with the
Bridges family, the relatives of her brother's wife;
sometimes a day and night at the "White Friars"
in Canterbury—the home of Mrs. Thomas
Knight after her quitting Godmersham Park.
Writing of a visit to the latter place, Miss Austen
remarks: "It was a very agreeable visit. There
was everything to make it so—kindness, conversation, variety, without care or cost. Mr. Knatchbull from Provender, was at the White Friars

* "Letters," Lord Brabourne.

when we arrived and stayed dinner, which with Harriet,* who came, as you may suppose, in a great hurry, ten minutes after the time, made our number six. Mr. K. went away early; Mr. Moore succeeded him, and we sat quietly working and talking till ten, when he ordered his wife away and we adjourned to the dressing-room to eat our tart and jelly." The next morning Mrs. Knight "had a sad headache which kept her in bed," but Jane, after paying some calls, returns to find her up and better; "but early as it was—only twelve o'clock," she continues, "we had scarcely taken off our bonnets before company came—Lady Knatchbull and her mother; and after them succeeded Mrs. White, Mrs. Hughes, and her two children, Mr. Moore, Harriet and Louisa, and John Bridges, with such short intervals between any as to make it a matter of wonder to me that Mrs. K. and I should ever have been ten minutes alone, or have any leisure for comfortable talk, yet we had time to say a little of everything. Edward came to dinner, and at eight o'clock he and I got into the chair, and the pleasures of my visit concluded with a delightful drive home."

If the engagements did not happen to furnish much amusement in themselves Miss Austen managed to get entertainment out of them in another way.

* Harriet Bridges, lately married to the Rev. George Moore.

MRS. THOMAS KNIGHT

Godmersham

" ''Tis night! and the landscape is lovely no more,' " she writes, " but to make amends for that, our visit to the Tyldens is over. My brother, Fanny, Edward, and I went; George stayed at home with W. K. There was nothing entertaining or out of the common way. We met only Tyldens and double Tyldens. A whist-table for the gentlemen, a grown-up musical young lady to play at backgammon with Fanny, and engravings of the colleges at Cambridge for me. . . . Lady Elizabeth Hatton and Anna Maria called here this morning. Yes, they called; but I do not think I can say anything more about them. They came, and they sat, and they went."

" It seems now quite settled," she writes, " that we go to Wrotham on Saturday, the 13th (Nov.) spend Sunday there and proceed to London on Monday. I like the plan. I shall be glad to see Wrotham." *

The Rev. George Moore was Rector of the beautiful village of Wrotham which lies among the western Kentish hills. His wife was a sister-in-law of Edward Knight. We like to fancy Jane attending service in the fine old church on the village green or, perhaps, climbing Wrotham hill to trace the line of the old Pilgrims' route as it winds along the valley marked by its dark yew trees.

* " Letters," Lord Brabourne.

CHAPTER XIX

LONDON

" The flood of human life in motion."

Miss Jane Austen's acquaintance with London began at an early date, as she frequently passed a few days there when journeying between Hampshire and Kent.

We have mentioned her sleeping at an inn in Cork Street in 1796. Most of the coaches from the south and west of England set down their passengers, it seems, at the "White Horse Cellar " in Piccadilly, which stood near to the entrance of what is now the Burlington Arcade. Jane and her brothers, therefore, probably alighted here and they would find Cork Street, immediately behind the " White Horse Cellar," a convenient place for their lodging. The Bristol Hotel, whose name suggests its connection with the west, was probably their inn.

" Sense and Sensibility " was, as yet, unwritten in 1796, and we can imagine the future author taking note of the various localities in the neighbourhood which she afterwards introduced into her story. Sackville Street is close by, in which she placed the shop of Mr. Gray, the jeweller at whose counter Elinor and Marianne were kept waiting whilst the coxcomb Robert Ferrars was giving elaborate directions for the design of a toothpick case. "At last the affair was decided. The ivory, the gold, and the pearls, all received their appointment, and the gentleman having named the last day on which his existence could be continued without the possession of the tooth-pick case, drew on his gloves with leisurely care, and bestowing a glance on the Miss Dashwoods which seemed rather to demand, than express, admiration, walked off with a happy air of real conceit and affected indifference."

This same Mr. Gray's shop figures in another well-known novel of the period—namely, in the "Absentee" by Maria Edgeworth. And there we again meet with a coxcomb—Colonel Heath-cock, who is playing *personage muet* whilst his bride-elect, the Lady Isabel, and her mother, Lady Dashfort, are "holding consultation deep with the jeweller."

Mr. Gray, we find, was a real personage, for his name appears in the London Directory for 1814, where he is entered as "Mr. Thomas Gray, jeweller, 41, Sackville Street, Piccadilly."

Near at hand is Conduit Street, where the

Jane Austen

Middletons lodged, and, at no very great distance is Berkeley Street, leading out of Portman Square, where Mrs. Jennings' house stood in which Elinor and Marianne visited her. The Miss Steeles, we remember, stayed in a less elegant part of the town—namely in Bartlett's Buildings, Holborn. These Buildings are still to be seen, forming a quaint alley of dark brick houses with pedimented doorways and white window-frames. We have looked up at the windows and wondered behind which of them Edward Ferrars had his momentous interview with the avaricious Lucy, while her sister Nancy made "no bones" of listening at the keyhole to their conversation.

In 1811 Miss Jane Austen was in town, visiting her brother Henry and his wife in Sloane Street. Henry had married his widowed cousin, Madame de Feuillade, who, the reader may remember, was much at Steventon parsonage during Jane's girlhood. A few years later Miss Austen was visiting her brother in Hans Place, a turning out of Sloane Street. All that district then formed a rural suburb of London.

Miss Mitford, who has so often helped us to realise the surroundings of Jane Austen, comes to our aid again here. She is describing the view of London, as seen a few years earlier, from the top of St. Paul's :—"I saw," she says, "a compact city, spreading along the river it is true, from

London

Billingsgate to Westminster, but clearly defined to the north and to the south; the West End beginning at Hyde Park Corner, and bordered

BARTLETT'S BUILDINGS, HOLBORN

by Hyde Park on the one side and the Green Park on the other. . . . Belgravia was a series of pastures, and Paddington a village." And we are also told " that Hans Place" was then " nearly surrounded by fields." Miss Austen, indeed, in a letter written from Sloane Street, speaks of "walking into London" to do her shopping.

Jane saw much pleasant society while visiting the Henry Austens. She writes from Sloane Street of an evening party which had taken place on a certain Tuesday in April : "Our party went off extremely well. The rooms were dressed up with flowers, &c., and looked very pretty. . . . At half-past seven arrived the musicians in two hackney coaches and by eight the lordly company began to appear. Among the earliest were George and Mary Cooke, and I spent the greatest part of the evening very pleasantly with them. The drawing-room being soon hotter than we liked, we placed ourselves in the connecting passage, which was comparatively cool, and gave us all the advantage of the music at a pleasant distance, as well as that of the first view of every new comer. I was quite surrounded by acquaintance, especially gentlemen."

We are told that the music was "extremely good" and that it "included the glees of 'Rosabelle,' 'The Red Cross Knight,' and 'Poor Insect.'" The "harp-player was Wiepart," Jane writes, "whose name seems famous though new to me." There was one female singer, "a short Miss Davis, all in blue, bringing up for the public line, whose voice was said to be very fine indeed."

London

We hear of an evening spent with some French emigrés—the D'Entraigues and Count Julien, friends of " Eliza " (Mrs. Henry Austen) and we learn that " Monsieur, the old Count " was " a very fine-looking man with quiet manners " and was evidently " a man of great information and taste." " He has some fine paintings," Jane remarks, " which delighted Henry ; and among them a miniature of Philip V. of Spain, Louis XIV.'s grandson, which exactly suited *my* capacity. Count Julien's [musical] performance is very wonderful." *

Mrs. Henry Austen died in 1813, and the house in Sloane Street was soon afterwards given up. Henry was at that time a partner in Tilson's Bank, which stood in Henrietta Street, Covent Garden, and he probably had rooms at the bank for there his sister Jane and their niece Fanny Knight visited him in the spring of 1814.

In the early summer of that year Jane was at Chawton again, and her sister Cassandra was in town. This was during an exciting time in London, for the Allies, having just established Louis XVIII. on his throne, were meeting together in London for a Thanksgiving service at St. Paul's, to be followed by a series of grand fêtes and entertainments. Jane writes to her sister on the 13th of June : " Take care of yourself, and do not be trampled to

* " Letters," Lord Brabourne.

Jane Austen

death in running after the Emperor. The report in Alton yesterday was that they would certainly travel this road either to or from Portsmouth." Amongst the Allies the Emperor Alexander (of Russia) was especially popular, and we have heard from an eye-witness that such was the enthusiasm of the crowds when he entered London, that they pressed round him to kiss his horse!

By the month of August Henry Austen had taken a house in Hans Place, No. 23, whence we find Jane writing to her sister, "It is a delightful place—more than answers my expectation," and she goes on to speak in praise of the garden.

At the very next house, No. 22, was the school, already mentioned in these pages, which had been started by Monsieur and Madame St, Quintin as a successor to the Reading Abbey School. There, as we have seen, Miss Mitford received her education, and there she frequently returned for visits in after life. From her we learn that the school had a good garden behind it adjoining the grounds of a mansion called the Pavilion; and from Jane herself we learn that on the further side there was another garden, belonging to No. 24, a house in which Mr. Tilson, of Tilson's Bank, resided.

In the summer of which we are writing Miss Mitford spent a fortnight in Hans Place, and she writes to her mother describing a visit to Lady

London

Charlotte Dennis's grounds belonging to the Pavilion whose entrance gates were in Hans Place. "What do you think," she asks, "of a dozen different ruins, half a dozen pillars, ditto urns, ditto hermitages, ditto grottoes, ditto rocks,

HOUSES IN HANS PLACE

ditto fortresses, ditto bridges, ditto islands, ditto live bears, foxes and deer, with statues wooden, leaden, bronze, and marble past all count? What do you think of all this crammed into a space of about ten acres, and at the back of Hans Place? It is really incredible. Mr. Dubster's villa is nothing to it." There is an allusion, by the way, to this same Mr. Dubster (a character in Fanny Burney's "Camilla") and to his summer house in one of Miss Austen's early letters.

We hear of frequent visits to the theatre in the "Letters" from London. Jane goes with her brother and her niece Fanny to see "Mr. Kean as 'Shylock' at Drury Lane," and writes afterwards to her sister, "I shall like to see Kean again excessively, and to see him with you too. It appeared to me as if there were no fault in him anywhere; and in his scene with 'Tubal' there was exquisite acting." She tells us that she saw "the new Mr. Terry" as "Lord Ogleby" and that "Henry thinks he may do" and mentions Young in "Richard III." at Covent Garden. "We were all at the play last night," she writes, "to see Miss O'Neil in 'Isabella.' I do not think she is quite equal to my expectations. I fancy I want something more than can be. I took two pocket-handkerchiefs but had very little occasion for either. She is an elegant creature, however. . . . We went to the Lyceum and saw the 'Hypocrite' an old play taken from Molière's 'Tartuffe,' and were well entertained. Dowton and Mathews were the good actors ; . . . I have no chance of seeing Mrs. Siddons. . . . I should particularly have liked seeing her in 'Constance.'" Sometimes when the younger children from Godmersham happen to be in town "Aunt Jane" takes them to see a play. "They revelled last night," she writes, "in 'Don Juan.' . . . We had scaramouch and a ghost, and were delighted."

Apropos of London shopping, Jane speaks of having some "superfluous wealth" to spend. Was it, we wonder, from the proceeds of "Sense and Sensibility"? "I hope," she writes to her sister, "that I shall find some poplin at Layton and Shear's that will tempt me to buy it. If I do it shall be sent to Chawton, as half will be for you; for I depend upon your being so kind as to accept it . . . It will be a great pleasure to me. Don't say a word. I only wish you could choose it too. I shall send twenty yards."* Layton and Shear's shop, we find, was at 11, Henrietta Street, Covent Garden.

One day Jane orders a cap for herself. "It will be white satin and lace," she writes, "and a little white flower perking out of the left ear, like Harriet Byron's feather." Fanny buys "Irish" at Newton's in Leicester Square, and stockings at Remmington's; "silk at 12s. a pair, and cotton at 4s. 3d.," which are thought to be "great bargains" —and the aunt and niece choose "net for Anna's gown at Grafton House," which is so thronged that they have to wait full half an hour before they can be attended to, "Edward sitting by all the time with wonderful patience."

In one of her "Letters" she speaks of going to

* "Letters," Lord Brabourne.

the Liverpool Museum and to the British Gallery. "I had some amusement at each," she writes, "though my preference for men and women always inclines me to attend more to the company than the sight." Does not this remind us of Elizabeth Bennet's pleasure in studying character? In returning home from her expeditions Jane is sometimes alone in her brother's carriage. "I liked my solitary elegance very much," she says, "and was ready to laugh all the time at my being where I was. I could not but feel that I had naturally small right to be parading about London in a barouche." Was she thinking of her own situation, we wonder, when she made Mrs. Elton talk of Selina's "being stuck up in the barouche-landau without a companion"?

In all the "busy idleness" of her London visits Miss Austen's mind turned constantly to the subject of her books. "Lady Robert is delighted with P. and P.," she writes, "and really *was* so, as I understand, before she knew who wrote it, for, of course she knows now. . . . And Mr. Hastings! I am quite delighted with what such a man writes about it. Let me be rational," she exclaims, "and return to my full stops." And she goes on to describe her brother Henry's plans concerning a visit to Chawton. "Mansfield Park," had only been published a few months when Jane wrote (Nov. 18th, 1814) "You will be glad to hear that the first edition of M. P. is all sold." And she goes on to say that Henry advises her making arrangements with the publisher for a second edition.

We hear of a small evening party to be given in Hans Place whilst Fanny is staying there with her aunt. After describing the morning engagements, Jane writes : "Then came the dinner and Mr. Haden, who brought good manners and clever conversation. From seven to eight the harp ; at eight Mrs. L. and Miss E. arrived, and for the rest of the evening the drawing-room was thus arranged: on the sofa the two ladies, Henry and myself, making the best of it ; on the opposite side Fanny and Mr. Haden, in two chairs (I *believe*, at least, they had *two* chairs), talking together uninterruptedly. Fancy the scene ! And what is to be fancied next ? Why that Mr. H. dines here again to-morrow. . . . Mr. H. is reading 'Mansfield Park' for the first time, and prefers it to P. and P." *

During a visit to her brother in 1815 Jane was engaged in correcting the proof sheets of "Emma." Writing on November 20th she remarks : "The printers continue to supply me very well, I am advanced in vol. iii. to my *arra-*root, upon which peculiar style of spelling there is a modest query in the margin." This is, of

* "Letters," Lord Brabourne.

Jane Austen

course, an allusion to Emma's sending the arrow-root to Jane Fairfax which Jane so promptly declined.

It was in connection with " Emma " that Miss Austen received the only distinguished mark of recognition that ever reached her. Mr. Austen Leigh tells us : " It happened thus. In the autumn of 1815 she nursed her brother Henry through a dangerous fever and slow con-valescence at his house in Hans Place. He was attended by one of the Prince Regent's physicians." Although " her name had never appeared on a title-page all who cared to know might easily learn it, and the friendly physician was aware that his patient's nurse was the author of ' Pride and Prejudice.' Accordingly he in-formed her one day that the Prince was a great admirer of her novels : that he read them often, and kept a set in every one of his residences." On hearing that " Miss Austen was staying in London the Prince had desired Mr. Clarke, the librarian of Carlton House, to wait upon her. The next day Mr. Clarke made his appearance, saying that he had the Prince's instructions to show her the library and other apartments, and to pay her every possible attention." During her visit to Carlton House " Mr. Clarke declared him-self commissioned to say that if Miss Austen had any other novel forthcoming she was at liberty to dedicate it to the Prince. Accordingly such a dedication was immediately prefixed to 'Emma,' which was at that time in the press."

A pleasant correspondence ensued between Miss Austen and Mr. Clarke, given in the "Memoir." In answer to some warm expressions of admiration for her works, she writes : "I am too vain to wish to convince you that you have praised them beyond their merits. My greatest anxiety is that this fourth work should not disgrace what was good in the others. . . . I am strongly haunted with the idea that to those readers who have preferred 'Pride and Prejudice' it will appear inferior in wit, and to those who have preferred 'Mansfield Park' inferior in good sense."

Mr. Clarke ventured to suggest a subject to be be treated of in her next work—that of the character of a clergyman of an enthusiastic turn of mind, "demurely sad, like Beatie's Minstrel." Jane modestly declines the proposal declaring that she could not do justice to his clergyman unless she possessed a wide acquaintance with classical literature, "and I think," she concludes, "I may boast myself to be with all possible vanity, the most unlearned and uninformed female who ever dared to be an authoress." But Mr. Clarke was by no means discouraged, and he proposed another subject, suggested to his mind by the approaching marriage of the Princess Charlotte and Prince Leopold—namely "An historical romance illustrative of the august House of Coburg." Again Jane declines, observing, playfully, " I could not sit seriously down to write a serious romance under any other motive than to save my life ; and if it were indispensable for me to keep it up and never to relax into laughing at myself or at other people, I am sure I should be hung before I had finished the first chapter."

Charlotte Brontë received similar suggestions and repudiated them with stern eloquence, very different from Jane Austen's "playful raillery." Miss Mitford too did not escape from such counsels, for she was urged to write a poem on the Battle of Copenhagen, which she promptly refused to do, declaring that she was "totally unfit for such an undertaking," and adding, " I do not think I would write upon it even if I could. Cobbett * would never forgive me for such an atrocious offence, and I could not offend him to please all the poets in the kingdom." The answers are very characteristic of the three writers.

* Cobbett was an intimate friend of her father.

CHAPTER XX

CHAWTON

*"Her ready fingers plied with equal skill
The needle or the quill."*

WE will now follow Miss Austen once more to her Chawton home—the cottage from which all her works were sent out into the world.

Busy as she is with her own compositions we find her lending a helping hand to her niece Anna, who is writing a novel herself—her first effort of so important a nature. As each chapter is completed it is forwarded to the kind Aunt for her advice and criticism, and these, conveyed in letters to Anna, reveal, though in her own playful way, many of Miss Austen's serious views as to a right standard of style and composition. They show us also, incidentally, how careful she was herself to be correct in topographical and other statements.

These letters, which have already appeared in Lord Brabourne's work, have been lent to us in the MS., and it is from the MS. that we now quote.

Jane Austen

Writing in the early summer of 1814, Jane thanks her niece for an instalment of her novel just arrived which "has entertained" her "extremely." "I read it aloud," she goes on to say, "to your grandmamma and Aunt Cass, and we were all very much pleased. . . . A few verbal corrections are all that I feel tempted to make—the principal of them is a speech of St. Julian to Lady Helen, which you see I have presumed to alter. . . . I do not like a lover speaking in the third person ; it is too much like the formal part of Lord Orville,* and *I* think it not natural. If *you* think differently, however, you need not mind me." And again she writes : " Let the Portmans go to Ireland, but as you know nothing of the manners there you had better not go with them. You will be in danger of giving false representations. Stick to Bath and the Foresters. There you will be quite at home . . . Lyme will not do. Lyme is towards forty miles from Dawlish, and would not be talked of there. I have put Starcross instead. If you prefer Exeter that would be always safe. [Lady Clanmurray and her daughter] must be two days going from Dawlish to Bath. They are nearly one hundred miles apart.

". . . Your Aunt C. does not like desultory novels, and is rather afraid yours will be too

* The hero of Fanny Burney's " Evelina."

much so. . . . It will not be so great an objection
to me if it is. I allow much more latitude than
she does, and think nature and spirit cover many
sins of a wandering story.

". . . What can you do with Egerton to increase
the interest for him? I wish you could contrive
something. . . . Something to carry him myste-
riously away and then (be) heard of at York or
Edinburgh in an old great coat. . . . Devereux
Forester's being ruined by his vanity is extremely
good, but I wish you would not let him plunge
into 'a vortex of dissipation.' I do not object
to the thing, but I cannot bear the expression ; it
is such thorough novel slang, and so old that I
daresay Adam met with it in the first novel he
opened."

During the time that Anna Austen was occupied
in writing this story she became engaged to be
married to Mr. Benjamin Lefroy, a son of
"Madame" Lefroy, of Ashe, to whom Jane was so
much attached, and who was killed by a fall from
her horse in 1804.

"St. Julian's history was quite a surprise to
me," Miss Austen writes, "you had not very long
known it yourself I expect; but I have no objection
to make to the circumstance, and it is very well
told. His having been in love with the aunt
gives Cecilia an additional interest with him.
I like the idea—a very proper compliment to an

aunt! I rather imagine indeed that nieces are seldom chosen but out of compliment to some aunt or another. I daresay Ben was in love with me once, and would never have thought of you if he had not supposed me dead of scarlet fever."

" Waverley " had been published in the month of July of this same year (1814), and Miss Austen writes to her niece in the following September : "Walter Scott has no business to write novels, especially good ones. It is not fair. He has fame and profit enough as a poet, and should not be taking the bread out of other people's mouths. I do not like him, and do not mean to like 'Waverley' if I can help it—but fear I must."

It is amusing to see how Jane Austen's woman's wit enabled her to solve at once the mystery of the "Great Unknown," when even Scott's most intimate friends were fairly puzzled. Lord Jeffrey writes: "Though living in familiar intercourse with Sir Walter, I need scarcely say that I was not in the secret of his authorship ; and, in truth, had no assurance of the fact till the time of its public promulgation." This promulgation was in February 1827.

The marriage of Anna Austen and Benjamin Lefroy took place at Steventon on November 8, 1814. For those who may be interested to hear how a wedding was conducted nearly ninety years ago, we quote a few passages from an account of it written by a younger sister of the bride.*

"Weddings were then," she remarks, "usually very quiet. The old fashion of festivity and publicity had quite gone by, and was universally condemned as showing the bad taste of all former generations. . . . This was the order of the day.

"The bridegroom came from Ashe, where he had hitherto lived with his brother (the Rector), and with him came Mr. and Mrs. Lefroy, and his other brother, Mr. Edward Lefroy ; Anne Lefroy, the eldest little girl, was one of the bridesmaids, and I was the other. We wore white frocks and had white ribbon in our straw bonnets. . . . My brother† came from Winchester that morning, but was to stay only a few hours. We in the house had a slight early breakfast upstairs, and between nine and ten the bride, my mother, Mrs. Lefroy, Anne, and myself were taken to church in our carriage. All the gentlemen walked." The bride, who was very pretty, wore, we are told, "a dress of fine white muslin, and over it a soft silk shawl, white shot with primrose, with embossed white-satin flowers, and very handsome fringe, and on her head a small cap to match, trimmed with lace."

The writer speaks of the "cold grey light of a

November morning" making its way "through the narrow windows of the old church." " Mr. Lefroy," she continues, " read the service, and my father gave his daughter away. No one was in the church but ourselves, and no one was asked to the breakfast, to which we sat down as soon as we got back. The breakfast was such as best breakfasts then were. Some variety of bread, hot rolls. buttered toast, tongue, ham and eggs. The addition of chocolate at one end of the table and the wedding-cake in the middle marked the speciality of the day. . . . Soon after the breakfast the bride and bridegroom departed. They had a long day's journey before them to Hendon. . . . In the evening the servants had cake and wine. Such were the wedding festivities at Steventon in 1814."

In later years a daughter of the bride, commenting upon the extreme simplicity of these " festivities " observes " when Aunt Jane marries Emma Woodhouse (the heiress of thirty thousand pounds) she describes a wedding, which could not have been very different, and which Mrs. Elton, no doubt justly, thought very inferior to her own, and stigmatised as having 'very little white satin, very few .lace veils,' and summed up as being 'a most pitiful business.'"

Mrs. Benjamin Lefroy did not neglect her writing upon her marriage as Mrs. Elton did her music, but continued to send her MS. as it progressed to her aunt. Miss Austen writes in December of the same year (1814): " I have been very far from thinking your book an evil, I assure you. I read it immediately and with great pleasure. . . . Indeed I think you get on very fast. I only wish other people of my acquaintance could compose as rapidly."

But as time went on and the cares of a family intervened, the story was put aside for a season, and before it could be resumed the beloved Aunt had passed away. " With no Aunt Jane to read, to criticise, and to encourage," writes Mrs. Lefroy's daughter, "it was no wonder that the MS., every word of which was so full of her, remained untouched. . . . The story was laid by for years, and then one day, in a fit of despondency, burnt. I remember," she continues, "sitting on the rug watching its destruction, amused with the flame and the sparks which kept bursting out in the blackened paper. In later years, when I expressed my sorrow that my mother had destroyed her story she said she could never have borne to finish it." *

Miss Lefroy tells us that her father and mother, remained at Hendon until August 1815, when they removed to a house called Wyards, near to Alton. " It was a large farmhouse," she says, "one end of which was occupied by a sort of bailiff or

* Family MSS.

Jane Austen

foreman with his family, and they rented the remainder. The intercourse between the two cottages, as we may call them, was almost daily, and the correspondence between the aunt and niece nearly ceased."

It happened at this time that Miss Austen was enjoying the society of several members of her family : for her brother Edward and his many children were at the " Great House," whilst Francis and his family were residing for a while in the neighbourhood—" sweet amiable Frank," as she calls him. The Captain had recently returned to England after serving in the eventful campaigns of the North Sea and Baltic.

Charles was the only brother who was far away. He had been sent in command of three ships to the Mediterranean on the escape of Napoleon from the Isle of Elba. "Thank you," Jane writes to her sister, "for the sight of dearest Charles' letter to yourself. How pleasantly and how naturally he writes! and how perfect a picture of his disposition and feelings his style conveys!"

When peace was restored, after the battle of Waterloo, we hear of Captain Charles Austen waging war against the pirates of the Archipelago, capturing their vessels and putting an end to their cruel trade. The following year his ship, the *Phœnix*, was wrecked during a hurricane off

THE OAK-ROOM IN CHAWTON HOUSE

Chawton, Friday Sept. 29.
1615

My dear Anna

We we told Mr. B. Lefroy that if the weather did
not prevent us, we should certainly come & see you tomorrow,
& bring Cassy, trusting to your being so good as to give her
a Dinner about one o'clock, that we might be able to
be with you the earlier & stay the longer — but on going
to Cassy the choice of the Fair or a Ride, it must be confessed
that she preferred the former, which we trust will not
greatly offend you; — if it does, you may hope that some
little Anna hereafter may revenge the insult by avowing a
preference of an Alton Fair. As her Cousin Cassy — So this
meanwhile, we have determined to put off our visit to
you till Monday, which we hope we shall be not left
convenient to you. I wish the weather may not [...]

[...]

therefore should appear too dirty for walking, & M.B.
L. would be so kind as to come & fetch me &
spend some part of the morn! with you, I
should be much obliged to him. Coppy knight
_

... of the Party ~ & your Aunt La pardonnerai de
faire another opportunity. —

Your G. Mama sends her Love & thanks for your
note. she was very happy to hear the contents of your
Parting Coe. the wife sends the strawberry roots
by Sally Bourdown, as early not weeds as the
weather may allow her to Parkesthon &c. —

                    Yours very affec.ly

                    My dear Emma

                            J. Austen

Chawton

the coast of Smyrna. The disaster happened near
to Chisnié on February 21 (1816), and is recorded
in true sailor fashion in the captain's journal,
of which we possess an extract: "At 2 P.M.,"
he writes, "the ship struck on the rocks astern,
it then blowing a gale from the north-east. Hoisted
out boats and cut the masts away. Attempted to
heave the ship off . . . rudder broken and washed
away. . . . The people immediately began to
swim on shore, all the boats being stove. At
4 P.M. a Turk, with a message from the Aga,
came down opposite the ship and inquired for me,
when I landed, sliding down on a top-gallant mast,
which reached from the wreck to the shore.
Thank God, I found that no life had been lost.
Walked to the town with the marine officer and
others, distant a long mile, blowing violently, with
sleet and rain, and very cold. At the house of
Mr. Cortovitch we were received most kindly and
hospitably, in supplying us with clothes, food,
and beds. For the crew I got a large store-house
with fires, bread, and wine. In spite of our
misfortune I slept well."

Whilst all these stirring events were taking
place, Jane was seated at her desk in the little
parlour of Chawton Cottage, writing of Anne
Elliot and of Captain Wentworth. In a letter to
her niece Fanny, dated March 13 (1816), we find
these words: "I *will* answer your kind questions

Jane Austen

more than you expect. 'Miss Catherine' is put upon the shelf for the present, and I do not know that she will ever come out; but I have a something ready for publication, which may, perhaps, appear about a twelvemonth hence. It is short —about the length of 'Catherine.' This is for yourself alone." The "something ready for publication" was, of course, "Persuasion," while "Catherine" refers to "Northanger Abbey."

We have spoken of Miss Austen's firm, delicate handwriting. One of her letters lies open before us. It is indited upon a square sheet of paper, such as was used in those days, and when refolded in its neat sharp creases, forms its own envelope. The writing beneath that part which makes the flap and takes the seal is very small. Every inch of space had to be made use of in order to save "double postage," which was then charged if a letter consisted of more than one sheet of paper.

Excellent as Jane's writing is, she herself considered it very inferior to that of her sister. "I took up your letter again," she writes, "and was struck by the prettiness of the hand, so small and so neat! I wish I could get as much into a sheet of paper."

"Jane Austen was successful in everything that she attempted with her fingers," writes Mr. Austen Leigh. "None of us could throw spilikins in so perfect a circle, or take them off with so steady a hand. Her performances with the cup-and-ball were marvellous. She has been known to catch the ball on the point above a hundred times in succession." The accompanying drawing is of an ivory cup-and-ball at Chaw-ton House, which was there in Miss Austen's time, and which, therefore, she must have frequently used.

Her needlework was exquisite. We have seen a muslin scarf embroidered by her in satin-stitch, and have held in our hands a tiny housewife of fairy-like proportions, which Jane worked at the age of sixteen as a gift for a friend. It consists of a narrow strip of flowered silk, embroidered at the back, which measures four inches by one and a quarter, and is furnished with minikin needles and fine thread. At one end there is a tiny pocket, containing a slip of paper upon which are some verses in diminutive handwriting with the date "Jany 1792." The little housewife, when rolled up, is tied with narrow ribbon. "Having been never used and carefully preserved, it is as fresh and bright as when it was first made."

CHAPTER XXI

AN EPISODE IN JANE AUSTEN'S LIFE

" He best can paint them who shall feel them most."

IT has been generally assumed by Jane Austen's numerous critics that, in spite of her Shakespearean power of describing the feelings of lovers, she had never experienced those feelings herself. "Friendship," writes Lord Acton, "was enough for her. In it she, in fact, seems to have found sufficient tenderness and support to satisfy her cravings. . . . She sat apart in her rocky tower and watched the poor souls struggling in the waves beneath. And her sympathies were not too painfully engaged, for she knew that it was only an Ariel's magic tempest, and that no loss of life was to follow. . . . Accordingly, her view of the life she described was that of a humorist, but of a very kindly one."

And Mr. Austin Dobson remarks : " On the whole we may assume that Miss Austen had no definite romance of her own." If "in the words of the French song, ' L'amour a passé par

An Episode in Jane Austen's Life

là,' the marks of his footprints have now been irretrievably effaced." The writer attributes her long silence as an author—a silence lasting for twelve years, and whose cause has puzzled Miss Austen's biographers, to her disappointment at the ebuffs she had received from publishers.

Another critic writing upon "Miss Austen and Miss Mitford,"* says : "We are absolutely denied a love tale in both these lives, which is hard. . . . No man's existence could be more entirely free from sentiment. If love is a woman's chief business then here are two very sweet women who had no share in it. It is a want, but we have no right to complain. . . . Such a question, it is unnecessary to say, could not have been discussed by a contemporary, but the critic at this distance may be permitted to regret that there is not somewhere, a faded bunch of violets or some dead forget-me-nots, to be thrown with the myrtle and the bay of their country's appreciation, upon these two maiden graves."

But the same critic has the insight to perceive that between the composition of the first three novels, and the last three "some softening influence" had come over the writer. "It is not," he says, "that the force is less or the keenness of insight into all the many manifestations of foolishness, but human sympathy has come in to

* *Blackwood's Magazine* for March 1870.

sweeten the tale, and the brilliant intellect has found out somehow that all the laughable things surrounding it—beings so amusingly diverse in their inanity and unreason—are all the same mortal creatures with souls and hearts within them. How Miss Austen came to find this out we cannot tell. But it is pleasant to see that she made the discovery. In 'Emma' everything has a softer touch. The sun shines as it never shone over the Bennets."

In an article by Miss Lefroy that appeared in "Temple Bar" some years ago the writer tells us that a large number of Miss Austen's letters, dealing with matters of a private nature, were burnt after her death. She goes on to say: "With all the playful frankness of her manner, her sweet sunny temper and enthusiastic nature, Jane Austen was a woman most reticent as to her own deepest and holiest feelings; and her sister Cassandra would have thought she was sinning against that delicacy and reserve had she left behind her any record of them. . . . That, on the contrary, it was her duty to the public to preserve whatever could throw any light on her sister's life and character never occurred to her. . . . We feel ourselves aggrieved that we have lost so much, but if Jane Austen had been asked she would undoubtedly have approved of her sister's conduct."

An Episode in Jane Austen's Life

In spite of "scanty materials," however, Miss Lefroy has recorded, upon carefully weighed evidence, an episode in her Aunt Jane's life, which must be deeply interesting to all who admire and love Miss Austen's works. This episode, but faintly alluded to heretofore by the biographers, is recounted in some family papers from which we are allowed to quote.

"The Austens with their two daughters, were once travelling in Devonshire," writes Miss Lefroy, "moving from place to place; and I think that tour was before they left Steventon in 1801, perhaps as early as 1798 or 1799. It was whilst they were so travelling, according to Annt Cassandra's account, given many years afterwards, that they somehow made acquaintance with a gentleman of the name of Blackall (a clergyman). He and Aunt Jane mutually attracted each other, and such were his charms that even Aunt Cassandra thought him worthy of her sister. They parted on the understanding that he was to come to Steventon, but instead came, I know not how long after, a letter from his brother to say that he was dead. There is no record of Jane's affliction, but I think the attachment must have been very deep. Aunt Cassandra herself had so warm a regard for him that some years after her sister's death, she took a good deal of trouble to find out and see his brother." [This brother was

Jane Austen

a medical man, whose acquaintance the Austens had also made in Devonshire.]

Miss Lefroy here gives the following extract from a letter written by her aunt Caroline Austen.

"I have no doubt that Aunt Jane was beloved of several in the course of her life, and was herself very capable of loving. I wish I could give you more details as to Mr. Blackall. All that I know is this. At Newtown Aunt Cassandra was staying with us when we made the acquaintance of a certain Mr. Henry Edridge of the Engineers. He was very pleasing and very good looking. My aunt was much struck with him, and *I* was struck by her commendations, as she rarely admired any one. Afterwards she spoke of him as of one so unusually gifted with all that was agreeable, and said he had reminded her strongly of a gentleman they had met one summer when they were by the sea (I think she said in Devonshire), who had seemed greatly attracted by my Aunt Jane. That when they parted he was urgent to know where they would be the next summer, implying, or, perhaps, saying that he should be there also, wherever it might be. I can only say the impression left on Aunt Cassandra's mind was that he had fallen in love with Aunt Jane. Soon afterwards they heard of his death. I am sure she thought him worthy of her sister from the way

236

An Episode in Jane Austen's Life

she recalled his memory, and also that she did not doubt either that he would have been a successful suitor."

"I fancy it was about 1799," resumes Miss Lefroy, "that this blow fell upon Jane Austen, and to it and the similar sorrow that befell her beloved sister, I attribute the disuse of her pen during so many of the finest years of her life. Between her first novels and their successors there was a period of twelve years, a long strange silence for which there must surely have been some reason. Is it not probable that, lively and cheerful as she was in manner, she had that deep silent sorrow at her heart, which could not but indispose her to the exertion of writing, perhaps even paralysed the faculty of invention? 'Pride and Prejudice,' 'Sense and Sensibility,' and 'Northanger Abbey' were all written before she was five-and-twenty, indeed, I think we might say before she was three-and-twenty, and it was not until she was thirty-five that she began revising them for the Press. . . . That her grief should have silenced her is, I think, quite consistent with the reserve of her character. Many could have found consolation in pouring out their sorrows to the public, and describing their own feelings under the disguise of their heroines, but only once did Jane Austen's heart slip into her pen when she said, as Anne Elliot, 'all the privilege I claim for my sex, and it is not a very enviable one, is that of loving longest when hope is gone.'

"The similarity of their fates must have endeared the two sisters to each other, and made other sympathy unnecessary to either. No one was equal to Jane in Cassandra's eyes, and Jane looked up to Cassandra as to one far better and wiser than herself. They were, as their mother said, 'wedded to each other.' . . . Yet they had such a gift of reticence that the secrets of their respective friends were never betrayed. The young niece who brought her troubles to 'Aunt Jane' for advice and sympathy knew she could depend absolutely on her silence even to her sister. A strict fidelity which is, I think, somewhat rare between any two so closely united.

"There are many [persons] who find fault with Jane Austen's novels as hard and cold and prudish, and who think that such was her own nature—incapable of depth of feeling. . . . Of passionate feeling she was, perhaps, incapable, but passion is not depth, and still less is it long-lived. And as for the hardness and prudishness, I think there is not allowance enough made for the difference between the fashion in this matter in her day and our own. In hers people were called by their plain Christian names, and 'loves,' 'dears,' and 'darlings' were less plentifully used. Caresses were not so common and only bestowed in

An Episode in Jane Austen's Life

private. It is not only that her heroines abstain from ' throwing themselves into the arms of their lovers,' but as sisters they are equally reticent. Dear as Jane in ' Pride and Prejudice ' is to Lizzie, she is to her Jane, and Jane only ; and Elinor and Marianne, who in these days would have certainly been ' Nellie ' and ' Minnie ' are contented with their own names, unadorned with any prefix of affection. The only person she paints as addicted to the use of terms of endearment is Isabella Thorpe, who talks of her ' dearest, sweetest Catherine,' without having any real regard for her, or for any one else save herself. It is not feeling, but the expression of feeling which has altered. If we do not wear our hearts on our sleeves, we seem to keep them on our lips much more than formerly.

"It seems to me that the beauty of Jane Austen's character has been marred by the too careful suppression of the romance of her life. But, though I think it probably caused the long disuse of her pen, I do not mean to imply that it made her gloomy or discontented. She was bright and lively at home, and the delight of her little nephews and nieces. To my mother she was especially kind, writing for her the stories she invented for herself long ere she could write, and telling her others of endless adventure and fun, which were carried on from day to day, or from visit to visit. I have still in my possession, in Aunt Jane's writing, a drama my mother dictated to her, founded on 'Sir Charles Grandison,' a book with which she was familiar at seven years old."

We learn from Miss Lefroy that Miss Austen received an offer of marriage in 1802 from Mr. Bigg-Wither of Manydown Park, who is described as "a sensible pleasant man," and whose "sisters were already her friends." It would have been a match to give great satisfaction to the relatives on both sides, and from a worldly point of view highly advantageous to Jane. But she could not bring herself to consent to it, feeling probably that "the past was so dear to her, and her love" for him who was gone "so true and living" that it must make "any other attachment impossible."

CHAPTER XXII

LAST YEAR AT CHAWTON

*" Through every period of this changeful state
Unchanged thyself—wise, good, affectionate."*

WE have spoken of Miss Austen's being surrounded by many members of her family during
the year 1816. The little nephews and nieces
were eager visitors at the cottage. One of them
tells us how her " Aunt Jane " used to help them
in their games, and remarks : " She would furnish
us with what we wanted from her wardrobe ; and
would be the entertaining visitor in our make-
believe house. She amused us in various ways.
Once I remember in giving a conversation as
between myself and my two cousins, supposing
we were all grown up, the day after a ball."*

Here is a letter from Jane to the niece who
wrote the foregoing words. The " Cassy " mentioned, who was staying at Chawton Cottage,
was a child of Charles Austen—whose wife had
recently died. The letter is dated April 21
(1816).

* "Memoir," by J. E. Austen-Leigh.

Jane Austen

"MY DEAR CAROLINE.—. . . Cassy has had great pleasure in working *this*, whatever it may be, for you. I believe she rather fancied it might do for a quilt for your little wax doll, but you will find a use for it if you can I am sure. She often talks of you, and we should all be very glad to see you again, and if your papa * comes on Wednesday, as we rather hope, and it suited everybody that you should come with him, it would give us great pleasure. Our fair at Alton is next Saturday, which is also Mary Jane's † birthday, and you would be thought an addition on such a great day.

"Yours affec^ately

"J. AUSTEN." ‡

She alludes to little Cassy in another letter written a few months earlier to her niece Mrs. Ben. Lefroy, who, the reader may remember, was living with her husband at Wyards, a farmhouse near to Alton. "We told Mr. B. Lefroy," she remarks, "that if the weather did not prevent us we should certainly come and see you to-morrow and bring Cassy, trusting to your being good enough to give her a dinner about one o'clock, that we might be able to be with you the earlier and stay the longer ; but on giving Cassy her choice of the Fair or Wyards she has preferred the former, which we trust will not greatly affront

---

* Rev. James Austen.   † A child of Francis Austen.
‡ Family MSS.

Last Year at Chawton

you—if it does you may hope that some little Anna, hereafter, may revenge the insult by a similar preference of an Alton fair to her cousin Cassy."

About this time Mr. Lefroy took Holy Orders. The examination through which he had to pass was so different to those of our own times that

WYARDS

we will quote his daughter's account of it. "I have heard my mother say," she writes, "that when he returned from being ordained he told her that the Bishop had only asked him two questions—first, if he was the son of Mrs. Lefroy of Ashe, and, secondly, if he had married a Miss Austen. I suppose the chaplain's examination extended a little further but my impression is that having passed through Oxford was considered a sufficient guarantee of fitness, and that his questions were not much more troublesome than the Bishop's." *

In the early part of the year 1816 Jane Austen's health began gradually to decline. It is supposed that the strain of her brother Henry's illness—her anxiety and watchful nursing—had told upon her strength ; and she had been also tried in another way. The bank in which Henry was a partner had failed, owing to some commercial disasters of the time, and she had felt keenly for her brother in all that he had had to go through on this account. But her letters are cheerful as ever, and the allusions to her failing health few and far between and given only to allay the anxiety of her correspondents.

" I am almost entirely cured of my rheumatism," she writes to her niece, Fanny Knight, "just a little pain in my knee now and then to make me remember what it was, and keep on flannel. Aunt Cassandra nursed me beautifully." And a few weeks later she remarks, " I am got tolerably well again, quite equal to walking about and enjoying the air, and by sitting down and resting a good while between my walks I get exercise enough. I have a scheme, however, for accomplishing more, as the weather grows spring-like. I mean to take to riding the donkey ; it will be more

* Family MSS.

Last Year at Chawton

independent and less troublesome than the use of the carriage, and I shall be able to go about with Aunt Cassandra in her walks to Alton and Wyards."*

These very letters are full of affection and sweet playfulness, called forth by a circumstance connected with this same niece, namely, that she seemed likely, at that time, to become engaged to be married. Her aunt writes, "You are the delight of my life. Such letters, such entertaining letters as you have lately sent! such a description of your queer little heart! such a lovely display of what imagination does! You are worth your weight in gold, or even in the new silver coinage. You are so odd, and all the time so perfectly natural—so peculiar in yourself, and yet so like everybody else!

"I do not like that you should marry anybody. And yet I do wish you to marry very much . . . but the loss of a Fanny Knight will never be made up to me."

Two of Fanny's brothers were then staying at Chawton Cottage. "And now I will tell you," Jane continues, "that we like your Henry to the utmost, to the very top of the glass, quite brimful. . . . He does really bid fair to be everything his father and sister could wish; and William I love very much and so we do all; he is quite our

* "Letters," Lord Brabourne.

own William. In short we are very comfortable together ; that is we can answer for *ourselves.*" Here is an allusion to another brother of Fanny's who was on his way to Winchester School. "Charles and his companions passed through Chawton about nine this morning . . . Uncle Henry and I had a glimpse of his handsome face, looking all health and good humour."

She writes to Fanny on March 23 : "I took my first ride yesterday, and liked it very much. I went up Mounter's Lane and round by where the new cottages are to be, and found the exercise and everything very pleasant ; and I had the advantage of agreeable companions, as At. Cass, and Edward walked by my side. At. Cass is such an excellent nurse, so assiduous and unwearied ! But you know all that already."*

Soon after this letter was written Jane Austen paid a visit to her friends, the Fowles,† at Kintbury, in Berkshire. They noticed with concern that "her health seemed impaired, and observed that she went about her old haunts, and recalled old recollections connected with them in a particular manner, as if she did not expect ever to see them again." In one of her letters, after mentioning an attack of illness from which she had suffered, she remarks : " But I am getting too near complaint ;

---

* " Letters," Lord Brabourne.
† Mrs. Fowle was a sister of Mrs. James Austen.

it has been the appointment of God, however secondary causes may have operated." *

She rallied, however, once more, and later in the year we find her writing to her nephew Edward † in her old playful vein : "You will not pay us a visit yet, of course—we must not think of it. Your mother must get well first, and you must go to Oxford and *not* be elected ; after that a little change of scene may be good for you, and your physicians, I hope, will order you to the sea or to a house by the side of a very considerable pond." (This is an allusion to the horse-pond in the fork of the Winchester and Gosport roads in front of the cottage.) And again she writes : "I give you joy of having left Winchester. Now you may own how miserable you were there ; now it will gradually all come out, your crimes and your miseries—how often you went up by the mail to London, and threw away fifty guineas at a tavern ; and how often you were on the point of hanging yourself, restrained only, as some ill-natured aspersion upon poor old Winton has it, by the want of a tree within some miles of the city."

Her brothers, Henry and Charles, were both staying at the cottage at this time. Henry had recently been ordained. "They are each of

---

* "Memoir," by J. E. Austen-Leigh.
† Mr. Austen-Leigh.

them so agreeable in their different ways," she writes, " and harmonise so well that their visit is thorough enjoyment. Uncle Henry writes very superior sermons. You and I must try to get hold of one or two and put them into our novels : * it would be a fine help to a volume, and we could make our heroine read it aloud on a Sunday evening, just as well as Isabella Wardour in the 'Antiquary' is made to read the 'History of the Hartz Demon,' in the ruins of St. Ruth, though I believe, on recollection, Lovell is the reader. By the bye, my dear E., I am quite concerned for the loss your mother mentions in her letter. Two chapters and a half to be missing is monstrous! It is well that *I* have not been at Steventon lately, and therefore cannot be suspected of purloining them ; two strong twigs and a half towards a nest of my own would have been something. I do not think, however, that any theft of that sort would be really very useful to me. What should I do with your strong, manly, vigorous sketches, full of variety and glow ? How could I possibly join them on to the little bit (two inches wide) of ivory on which I work with so fine a brush as produces little effect after much labour ?" †

It is pleasant here to recall the well-known words of Sir Walter Scott, written in his diary for

---

* This nephew had been trying his hand at story-making.
† " Memoir."

Last Year at Chawton

March 14, 1826: "Read again for the third time, at least, Miss Austen's finely written novel of 'Pride and Prejudice.' That young lady had a talent for describing the involvements and feelings and characters of ordinary life which is to me the most wonderful I ever met with. The big bow-wow strain I can do myself like any now going; but the exquisite touch which renders ordinary commonplace things and characters interesting from the truth of the description and the sentiment, is denied to me."

As her health declined Jane Austen's habits of activity gradually ceased, and she was obliged to lie down much. "The sitting-room (at Chawton Cottage) contained only one sofa," Mr. Austen Leigh tells us, "which was frequently occupied by her mother, who was more than seventy years old. Jane would never use it, even in her mother's absence; but she contrived a sort of couch for herself with two or three chairs, and was pleased to say that this arrangement was more comfortable to her than a real sofa. Her reasons for this might have been left to be guessed, but for the importunities of a little niece, which obliged her to explain that if she herself had shown any inclination to use the sofa, her mother might have scrupled being on it so much as was good for her."

Jane Austen's mind did not share in this decay

of her bodily strength. "Persuasion" had been brought to an end in the month of July of this same year (1816), but the conclusion differed in treatment to that with which we are familiar: the re-engagement of the hero and heroine having been effected in a scene laid in Admiral Croft's lodgings. "Her performance, however," writes her nephew, "did not satisfy her. She thought it tame and flat, and was desirous of producing some-thing better. This weighed upon her mind . . , so that one night she retired to rest in very low spirits. But such depression was little in accordance with her nature, and was soon shaken off. The next morning she awoke to more cheer-ful views and brighter inspirations; the sense of power revived, and imagination resumed its course. She cancelled the condemned chapter, and wrote two others entirely different in its stead. . . . Perhaps it may be thought that she has seldom written anything more brilliant."

"In our judgment," writes an American critic, "there is no part in any of Miss Austen's novels that shows stronger marks of the hand of the consummate artist than the winding up of 'Persua-sion' and the natural, yet unexpected way in which the hero and heroine come out of the complications in which they have been entangled, and into the understanding which happily con-cludes the whole matter. The change from her first plan which is now made known to us, in this last effort of her genius, shows that her imagination was as vivid and her judgment as true as at any previous period of her authorship."*

In January 1817, Miss Austen wrote to a friend : "We have just had a few days' visit from Edward. . . . He grows still, and still improves in appearance, at least in the estimation of his aunts, who love him better and better, as they see the sweet temper and warm affections of the boy confirmed in the young man." It is to this same beloved nephew that we are indebted for the beautiful record of Jane Austen's life.

One of the last letters dated from Chawton that have been preserved is addressed to Jane's little niece, Cassy. It is written in text-hand, and is spelt backwards for the child's amusement. We give it spelt in the ordinary way :†

"MY DEAR CASSY,—I wish you a happy new year. Your six cousins came here yesterday, and had each a piece of cake. This is little Cassy's‡ birthday, and she is eight years old. Frank has begun learning Latin. Edward feeds the robin every morning. Sally often inquires after you. Sally Benham has got a new green gown.

---

* *Nation*, September 7, 1871.
† Family MSS.
‡ A child of Francis Austen.

Jane Austen

Harriet Knight comes every day to read to Aunt Cassandra. Good-bye, dear Cassy. Aunt Cassandra sends her love, and so do we all.

"Your affectionate Aunt,

"JANE AUSTEN."

CHAPTER XXIII

WINCHESTER

" A Christian's wit is inoffensive light,
A beam that aids, but never grieves the sight."

In the month of May (1817) Miss Austen was persuaded by her family to remove to Winchester in order to be under the care of a medical man of repute in the county—a member of the Lyford family. She and her sister Cassandra took lodgings in College Street.

Writing to her nephew Edward on May 27 she says : " Thanks to the kindness of your father and mother in sending me their carriage, my journey hither on Saturday was performed with very little fatigue, and had it been a fine day I think I should have felt none ; but it distressed me to see Uncle Henry and Wm. Knight, who kindly attended us on horseback, riding in the rain almost the whole way. . . . Our lodgings are very comfortable. We have a neat little drawing-room with a bow window overlooking Dr. Gabell's garden."

Jane Austen

We have followed Miss Austen to Winchester, and have visited the house in College Street where she passed the last weeks of her life. College Street is a narrow picturesque lane, with small old-fashioned houses on one side, terminating in the ancient stone buildings of the College. The garden ground on the opposite side of the street belonged, and still belongs, to the head master. We have entered the "neat little drawing-room with a bow window" which remains unchanged. It is a pretty quaint parlour, with a low ceiling and a narrow doorway. Its white muslin curtains and pots of gay flowers on the window sill lent a cheerful air to the room. We almost fancied we could see Miss Austen seated in the window writing to her nephew, glancing from time to time across the high-walled garden, with its waving trees, to the old red roofs of the Close, with the great grey Cathedral towering above them.

"On Thursday, which is a confirmation and a holiday," Jane writes, "we are to get Charles out to breakfast. We have had but one visit from *him*, poor fellow, as he is in the sick-room, but he hopes to be out to-night. We see Mrs. Heathcote every day." Mrs. Heathcote and her sister Miss Bigg (of Manydown) were residing in the Close.

She writes again later on: "I live chiefly on

"IN THIS HOUSE JANE AUSTEN SPENT HER LAST DAYS".

the sofa, but am allowed to walk from one room to the other. I have been out once in a sedan-chair, and am to repeat it and be promoted to a wheeled chair as the weather serves." And speaking of her illness she remarks, "On this subject I will only say further that my dearest sister, my tender watchful, indefatigable nurse has not been made ill by her exertions. As to what I owe to her, and to the anxious affection of all my beloved family on this occasion, I can only cry over it, and pray to God to bless them more and more." *

We are told by her brother Henry that "she supported, during two months, all the varying pain, irksomeness, and tedium," attendant on her decline "with more than resignation, with a truly elastic cheerfulness." "She retained," he says, "her faculties, her memory, her fancy, her temper, and her affections, warm, clear, and unimpaired, to the last. . . . She expired on Friday, July 18 (1817), in the arms of her sister."

On the 24th of that month she was buried in Winchester Cathedral. She lies in the north aisle, near to the old black marble font, and almost opposite to the beautiful chantry of William of Wykeham.

Cassandra writes to a niece on the day of the funeral, " I watched the little mournful procession

* " Memoir," by Henry Austen.

the length of the street ; and when it turned from my sight and I had lost her for ever, even then I was not overpowered, nor so much agitated as I am now in writing of it. Never was human being more sincerely mourned by those who attended her remains, than was this dear creature. May the sorrow with which she is parted with on earth be a prognostic of the joy with which she is hailed in heaven." *

.   .   .   .   .

The last picture we have of the Chawton home is of Cassandra living there alone after the death of both her mother and sister. "The small house and pretty garden," writes her niece, "must have been full of memories of them. She read the same books (that they had read) and kept in the little dining-room the same old piano on which her dear sister had played, and though gentle and cheerful and fond of her nephews and nieces . . . I am sure never thought any one of them to be compared in beauty and sweetness and goodness to her beloved Jane." "I remember," she continues, "when my mother and I were staying with her when I was about seventeen, being greatly struck and impressed by the way in which she spoke of her sister, there was such an accent of *living* love in her voice." †

* " Letters," Lord Brabourne.
† Family MSS.

THE PARLOUR IN COLLEGE STREET

Winchester

A short memoir of Jane Austen appeared early
in 1818 written by her brother Henry and prefixed to the first edition of "Northanger Abbey
and Persuasion." After speaking of the novels
he goes on to say that "In the bosom of
her own family their authoress talked of them
freely, thankful for praise, open to remark, and
submissive to criticism. But in public she turned
away from any allusion to the character of an
authoress. . . . No accumulation of fame would
have induced her, had she lived, to affix her
name to any productions of her pen. . . . It was
with extreme difficulty that her friends, whose
partiality she suspected, could prevail on her to
publish her first work. Nay, so persuaded was
she that its sale would not repay the expense of
publication, that she actually made a reserve from
her very moderate income to meet the expected
loss. She could scarcely believe what she termed
her 'great good fortune,' when 'Sense and
Sensibility' produced a clear profit of about
£150. . . . She regarded the above sum as a
prodigious recompense for that which had cost
her nothing." "Her power of inventing characters," he remarks, "seems to have been intui-
tive, and almost unlimited. She drew from
nature ; but whatever may have been surmised
to the contrary, never from individuals. . . .
She read aloud with very great taste and effect.

Jane Austen

Her own works, probably, were never heard to so much advantage as from her own mouth."

These words recall to our mind the incident of Jane's reading aloud the manuscript of "Mansfield Park" to this same brother, as they were travelling together in a post-chaise on their way to London.

After alluding to the popularity of some of the more sensational novels of the day, her brother continues : "The works of Jane Austen, however, may live as long as those which have burst on the world with more *éclat*. But the public has not been unjust, and our authoress was far from thinking it so."

Miss Austen's fame has been of slow growth, but it has steadily increased with the increase of culture. Even in her own day the best minds recognised her power, but now her works are enjoyed by thousands of readers who owe to her some of the happiest hours of their lives. Her critics too seem, each one, to find in her just those special qualities which he himself looks for in a favourite writer. One learned reviewer extols her adherence to the great principles of the literary art as acted upon by Homer and enforced by Aristotle, another praises her for her essentially feminine qualities, while a third is struck by her masculine vigour.

The American critic whom we have already

JANE AUSTEN'S GRAVE IN WINCHESTER CATHEDRAL

quoted remarks, "for the perfection of artifice which conceals itself, and seems nothing but the simplicity of nature and the necessary course of events, there is no story-teller that we know of that surpasses Jane Austen. Her stories never tire, and are as fresh in interest on the fiftieth reading as on the first, and her characters are as much actual entities to us as our own acquaintances, and much more so than most personages in history." Another critic dwells on what he calls her "dramatic ventriloquism," which makes us, "amid our tears of laughter and exasperation at folly, feel it almost impossible that she did not hear those very people utter those very words," so that "we are almost made *actors*, as well as spectators, of the little drama." Her "conversations," wrote Archbishop Whately, in 1821, "are conducted with a regard to character hardly exceeded by Shakespeare himself. Like him she shows as admirable a discrimination in the characters of fools as of people of sense." "Some persons," he tells us, "have declared that they have found her fools too true to nature, and consequently tiresome"; but of such persons he remarks that "whatever deference they may outwardly pay to received opinions," he is sure "they must find the 'Merry Wives of Windsor' and 'Twelfth Night' very tiresome."

A fourth critic remarks : "To have caused us

Jane Austen

an uninterrupted amusement without ever descending to the grotesque, to have been comic without being vulgar, and to have avoided extremes of every kind, without ever being dull or commonplace, is the praise of which Jane Austen is almost entitled to a monopoly." While another observes : " Even in Captain Price's case she did what Pope pronounced to be impossible, reconciled the 'tarpauline phrase' with the requirements of art and civility. Out of these bounds her language never strays. She is neat, epigrammatic, but always a lady."

Her power of what has been termed " describing without description " seems to us to be another monopoly of Miss Austen's. By a mere hint, dropped here and there, a whole character is placed before us. Who does not know Mrs. Rushworth by her "stately simper"? Or Mrs. Palmer by her spending her time in the London shops "in raptures and indecision"? Or Mr. John Knightley, who, when out of humour, was accustomed to have the sedative of " 'very true, my love' administered to him" by his wife? And who does not exactly comprehend the kind of intercourse between Mrs. Norris and Dr. Grant which "had begun in dilapidations"?

Her descriptions of nature, which are terse indeed compared with the elaborate "word-painting" of some of our writers, are reserved,

like those of Shakespeare, to increase the dramatic
effect of the situation. Take, for example, the
stormy wet July evening towards the end of
" Emma," which emphasises with its gloom
Emma's dismal forebodings. Or, take again
Anne Elliot's reflections during the walk to
Winthrop on that late autumnal day, upon declining happiness and the declining year, when the
sight of the ploughs busily at work on the uplands
brings a ray of hope showing that the farmers, at
any rate, " were meaning to have spring again."

In her description of places our authoress is
equally reticent, and yet with what consummate
power she places them before our eyes! One
of her critics writes : " It is impossible to con-
ceive a more perfect piece of village geography, a
scene more absolutely real " than " Highbury,
with Ford's shop in the High Street, and Miss
Bates's rooms opposite. . . . Nothing could be
more easy than to make a map of it, with indi-
cations where the London road strikes off, and by
which turning Frank Churchill, on his tired horse,
will come from Richmond. We know it as well
as if we had lived there all our lives and visited
Miss Bates every other day." *

In an article which appeared some years ago,
the writer concludes with the following remarks
upon Jane Austen : " Her fame, we think, must

* *Blackwood*, March 1870.

endure. Such art as hers can never grow old, never be superseded. But, after all, miniatures are not frescoes, and her works are miniatures. Her place is among the Immortals, but the pedestal is erected in a quiet niche of the great temple."

But we would remind this writer that "grandeur depends upon *proportion*, not size." A recent critic who maintains that Miss Austen's genius, in spite of apparently narrow limitations, had really ample scope, observes : " Ordinary life was seen by her not dimly and partially as we see it, but in all its actual vastness, and it was in this huge field that she worked with such supreme success. If the 'little bit of ivory' were only 'two inches wide' those inches were not of mortal measure."

No! for Ben Jonson has told us that—

> " In small proportions we just beauties see,
> And in short measures life may perfect be."

INDEX

INDEX

Index

Index

Index

Index

Index

Index

Index

Index